The
Cancerous
45th Presidency

A Failed Attempt at Martyrdom

Dennis Dawson Elliott

CHARTER
PUBLISHING

The Cancerous 45th Presidency:
A Failed Attempt at Martyrdom

© 2020 Dennis Dawson Elliott

ISBN: 978-0-578-76503-7 (p)

ISBN: 978-0-578-76504-4 (e)

Library of Congress Control Number: 2020918253

———————

Also by the author...
Armageddon of a Different Order
Wake Up, America
www.truthandethics.com
ISBN 978-1-5320-6201-8

*To the Founding Fathers whose wisdom, dedication
and foresight established the secure underpinnings for
our democracy and its adherence to the rule of law,
and to all those dedicated to its preservation.*

CONTENTS

INTRODUCTION

March 21, 1973 — "I think there's no doubt about the seriousness of the problem we've got. We have a cancer within–close to the presidency, that's growing. It's growing daily. It's compounding. It grows geometrically now, because it compounds itself."[1]

JOHN DEAN, WHITE HOUSE COUNSEL

On the day when John Dean spoke the above metaphor to President Richard Nixon in the Oval Office, he was attempting to get the president's attention in Dean's role serving as White House Counsel. He was offering a reality check for the president who Dean felt was out of touch with the growing ramifications of the Watergate break-in, Nixon's seemingly denial of all events, and the importance of what had and was transpiring. Dean was a first-line witness to the actions of members of the Nixon staff inner circle and perhaps he came to nervously observe the influence of these individuals on Nixon decisions. These decisions, and others, were facilitating an out of control situation that was fast escalating into a crisis for Nixon and the country, for which an appropriate and believable defense was becoming all but impossible.

The beginnings of formulating a plan for gathering intelligence on the Democratic opposition, thought to be useful and perhaps even necessary for Nixon's reelection campaign, had begun over a year earlier. Dean had far more information than Nixon was allowing himself to accept or that he even wanted to grasp. The cast of characters involved, including Dean himself as a coordinator of decisions, over time were being made by others in Nixon's inner circle. It may have become apparent, or suspected, to Dean that he was becoming a probable scapegoat for the growing cover-up of an intelligence operation that potentially he had perhaps unwillingly helped to create.

Not since the impeachment trial of Andrew Johnson had the country had to face a situation when its president came under such scrutiny, with 11 articles of impeachment approved by the House of Representatives in February 1868. Contributing to the notoriety of this point in history is the fact that Johnson had come to office following the assassination of President Abraham Lincoln and subsequently Johnson demonstrated a disregard for legislation that passed over his veto by taking actions regarding reconstruction of the Confederate States.[2] These steps precipitated an ideological political conflict and a comparison can be made today in the 21st century with President Donald Trump's attempts to both control and ignore the legislative branch of the government, including challenging Congressional oversight over the Executive Branch, attempts to use the Attorney General and the Department of Justice to achieve personal advantage, and his stabs at manipulating the judicial branch in its entirety.

The effort by Dean to secure Nixon's attention about an unbridled "disease" that was taking over his administration was admirable. Even though Dean was embroiled in the midst of the questionable activities of the Committee to Re-Elect the President[3] and the White House Plumbers Unit,[4] as well ongoing interactions with individuals in White House inner circle (*e.g.*, H.R. Haldeman, E. Howard Hunt, G. Gordon Liddy), Dean's distress gave way to responsible ethics and the interests of the country. Hoping individuals would come to realize that ethical behavior is not to be applied randomly or twisted to meet a preconceived agenda Dean, above all, chose to do what was right for the country and in the process right for himself. The treatment for the cancer he was describing to Nixon, and in this case not necessarily a cure for Dean, would not come easily as extraordinary circumstances were escalating all around him. Rather, he wanted to demonstrate to Nixon in that specific conversation in 1973 that a remission for the "cancer" in some form might be possible.

Gaining control of a confusing vortex of Nixon paranoia and decision making, as well as attempting to mediate events that were continuously occurring, presented a challenging task for Dean in light of the interactions with the broad cast of characters contributing to the disease inside and outside the White House. The situation was made even more difficult in light of the Nixon obsessive objective of pursuing a strategic and meaningful transition toward being re-elected. A magic bullet cure was not in the offing.

Author Evan Thomas in his book, *"Being Nixon: A Man Divided,"* has suggested that Nixon routinely demonstrated a spectrum of his deeply entrenched character. the polarity of Nixon's character. Thomas describes Nixon as "a man that was both a boisterous leader and a self-conscious manic, with the characteristics of the latter trait contributing to the president's personal and professional shortcomings."[5] It has also been speculated that Nixon may have been profoundly insecure because he wasn't part of the East Coast Republican establishment. He was a Whittier College *summa cum laude* graduate even though he had originally wanted to attend an Ivy League school. Later this may have morphed into a feeling of being "less than" his political opponents and not being accepted by the inside the DC beltway enterprise. Nevertheless, he proceeded to follow his path of thinking that only he could "fix" things and we have heard and seen these character traits and heard the same language from the 45th president as well.

Without question the primary and required component of Dean's objective of gaining civil control in the White house was persuading Nixon to let go of his anger and mistrust that combined to drive his day-to-day directions, also an easily identifiable trait of Trump. Almost from Nixon's initial inauguration in January 1969 the seeds of disorder of his presidency began to be revealed. He had inherited the conflict in Vietnam and understood that taking steps to win this war with any certainty would be difficult. Domestic opposition to the conflict and resulting economic and policy challenges contributed to the mindset of suspicion and obsessive manner on the part of the president. But there it was; these things came with the job. The cancer seeds were deeply planted in his presidency. In the case of Trump cancer, the seeds were about people, a vetting process for appointments and nominations for key positions that consisted of "gut feelings," friends over experience and the unspoken realization that Trump was not prepared or fit to be president.

For Nixon early symptoms of the disorder to come appeared in the form of the publication of the Pentagon Papers in June 1971. Released by Daniel Ellsberg, who was a military strategist employed by the Rand Corporation, the leaked material contained in the Papers precipitated a level of public focus and scrutiny on the Vietnam war that Nixon could not control or overcome. The Papers presented a history of the US political and military involvement in Vietnam that were first published in the *New York Times*, but not without a challenge from the president that ultimately resulted in a landmark ruling by the Supreme Court in 1971.[6] The essence of the challenge by the Nixon administration was to block further publication of the Papers by the Times and subsequently the *Washington Post,* citing the Espionage Act,[7] that related to unlawful disclosure of information affecting national defense. The Court's holding defended the First Amendment right of a free press against prior restraint (censorship) by the government. The open hostility toward the media, be it fact checking, fact reporting, or criticism of individuals and responsible watchdog journalism are shared trademarks of Nixon and Trump.

Another Nixon administration misguided reaction the same year was the formation of the Plumbers Unit in the White House in July. In hindsight this was the first and significant evidence of Nixon's mindset to take action against all those who he felt were obstructing him in numerous ways, particularly those who were leaking classified information. Thus, more early malignant cancer cells began to appear and from there they were to steadily proliferate. Once again, the cancer of the Nixon presidency is repeated in the Trump Oval Office though in the case of Trump it was a matter of consistently acting in ways that demonstrated that he was putting himself above the rule of law. Trump's consistent objection to any oversight of his policies and actions, firing of professionals who take their responsibilities seriously and thinking he had carte blanch to do whatever he wanted to do. It would just be unacceptable to this president for that not to be true.

In August of 1971 the infamous Nixon Enemies List[8] was formed, with those included on the list targeted using federal agency resources. It was a diverse list to be sure that of course included politicians but also journalists and even actors. The trail of questionable decisions continued in September when Ellsberg's psychiatrist's office was broken into by the Plumbers Unit in an attempt to uncover information to discredit Ellsberg and thus the Pentagon Papers. Trump's enemies list is considerably larger, made up of anyone who does not agree with him on any matter of policy or action and all those who are critical of him in any manner. This list never ends for Trump as criticism of his words and acts undoubtedly grows each day and thus new targets added for his bizarre complaints.

Early in 1972 the Plumbers began development of what became the plan for the break-in of the offices of the Democratic National Headquarters in the Watergate Hotel in DC in June of that year. In this same month, White House Chief of Staff H.R. Haldeman recommended to Nixon that the FBI investigation of the break-in be shut down. It has long been speculated that perhaps this recommendation may have been a catalyst for the type of thinking that became the cover-up that led to the final demise of the Nixon administration, and his resignation in August 1974 to avoid formal impeachment by the House of Representatives. The stonewalling of questions into the behaviors of Trump and his cronies may also foreshadow doom because of his continued deflections away from truth.

The period from the Watergate break-in arrests in June 1972 to Nixon's resignation was marked by Nixon's reelection to a second term in November and by numerous attempts by Nixon to ignore what had become increasingly obvious to the public. The cancer continued to grow as the Senate Watergate hearings were taking place: individuals came under scrutiny and some resigned, a special prosecutor was appointed, Archibald Cox, to exam potential presidential impropriety, Vice President Spiro Agnew resigned related to prior corruption during his time as governor of Maryland, the infamous "Saturday Night Massacre" occurred as Nixon ordered Attorney General Elliot Richardson to fire FBI Director William Ruckelshaus and the special prosecutor but both resigned. The parallels continue with Trump, but admittedly in a more clandestine way. His approach was dangling firings of individuals for a period of time until people resigned, with some exceptions to his own brand of HR methodology.

The cancer that Dean referred to had actually started to become apparent to him long before his testimony before the Senate Watergate Committee. Nixon's personality throughout his career showed little tendency to embrace compromise or accept expertise in areas far beyond his own. His ideas were not to be questioned, but respected and implemented. His ambition was guided by his obsession of never being wrong, his lack of trust of others and certainly no respect for the watchdog media. Observed this more recently? There are comparisons to be made between how Nixon had allowed himself to become embroiled in cancerous controversies and the characteristics of his actions during his time in office, and with Trump and his tumultuous administration. The peculiarities of the two presidents are shockingly similar: corrupt actions, attempts to cover-up misdeeds, lies, scandalous events and blaming others while accepting no responsibility. "The American people simply will not countenance being lied to by the president."[9] Unfortunately in the Trump era this does not seem to apply to many who continue to accept all of his obvious shortcomings, including being a liar of grand proportions.

Cancerous activity and growth can be revealed in many ways. In the Nixon administration there was a seminal source, the president himself. Today the White House has a resident that in many ways is a mirror image of that seminal source. There are equivalences revealed as the actions of Nixon and Trump are dissected for clarity. Nixon was faced with considerable challenges as he followed President Lyndon

Johnson into the White House. It was the hand he was dealt. Starting with his campaign and most days since Trump repeats and repeats that he inherited a mess that only he could fix. Facts don't support that claim as facts Trump don't associate well with each other. The country has seen how well his negativism has worked out for him. However, the growth of the cancer today is exponentially far more foreboding for the country's stability, the economic and personal health of its citizens at large and the US relationship with the global community.

Observing anyone fighting cancer is not enjoyable. Watching a country sink into despair while also witnessing governance by deceit provides a different type of pain and the decline of its stature and its democracy is nonetheless troublesome. Sporting event rhetoric, cheerleading and boastful lies at rallies just allows the Trump cancer to grow unrestrained. People ask what must happen to bring about a constructive recovery from the chaos and ineffectiveness of the Trump administration. How could this cancer debilitating the country have been avoided and now be excised? What therapies should be demanded to eliminate any ground for the further invasion and growth of the disease?

A country in a battle with a cancerous president can prevail. It will take leaders to lead, at all levels, and honesty above all. It will take citizens digging deep into an understanding that irreparable harm will occur in their lives without transformative change. The harm is not just a blip on the presidential radar of missteps. The harm currently being fostered on the American public will last for years even if Trump is not reelected. He is negatively impacting both political parties, contributes daily to the corrosive partisan divide that pervades the legislative branch, and even the obsessive control he chooses to exert over the Department of Justice and the judicial branch is a frightening prospect. The behavior of the Trump cancer has no boundaries.

What Dean never imagined at the time of his description of the cancer on the Nixon presidency was that the subsequent actions and outcomes while Nixon remained in office did not constitute a cancer cure. The Watergate hearings, release of the Oval Office tapes, administration staff and officials who were sent to jail, and the fallout from the subsequent President Gerald Ford pardon of Nixon were, in an historical sense, only a temporary "administration remission" of that cancer. But thanks to Dean and others who refused to jeopardize their integrity, decency, honesty and ethical principles the country was able to move on.

"The art of life is not controlling what happens to us but using what happens to us."

— GLORIA STEINEM —

Fast forward: Forty-three years after Nixon resigned in shame the next cancerous mutation arrived and began to escalate rapidly when Trump was elected president.

When I began to construct an outline for topics that I felt were important to cover in this book I was primarily focused on the divisive circumstances in which Americans find themselves today. The cancer metaphor seemed so very obvious to me as a framework for what I felt I wanted to explore and communicate to others. What I could not have anticipated at that time was that the country, and the world, would soon be facing an overwhelming health crisis situation, a pandemic, a sliding economy, a movement against police brutality, systemic racism and a president who encouraged negativity, violence and decidedly non-presidential responses across the board. The pandemic, as one example, was and is, a crisis that requires incredible leadership, cooperation, and management that would far exceed the response at the time of the 1918 influenza pandemic, or the deadly Ebola virus concentrated in West Africa decades later.

Full disclosure: I am able to put my thoughts on paper about the pandemic and the Trump administration response, with particular personal insights about medicine and research. I have had experience contributing to the design of protocols for testing of new drugs, the requirements and need for double-blind, placebo-controlled randomized studies to assess safety and efficacy of a new mediation for submission to the Food and Drug Administration (FDA). I understand why Phase IV post-marketing monitoring of side effects and other safety issues that were not significantly discovered during clinical testing must be reported to the FDA. I know why off-label prescribing (approved indications) and compassionate protocols are important for patient care. I recognize the importance of good manufacturing practices for providing rapid and safe production of medications and planning of distribution implementation. I have worked with renowned scientists and principal investigators in the US and around the world in evaluating pharmacology and toxicology studies prior to consideration of protocols for clinical trials in humans. I've learned about the HIV/AIDS epidemic in Kenya through on-the-ground experience in that country and saw the benefits of US support through the President's Emergency Plan for AIDS Relief (PEPFAR)[10] established during the administration of President George W. Bush in 2003.

From studying multiple tumor types in the field of oncology this work has provided me with a respect for innovative scientific study and the concomitant responsibilities of safety and efficacy evaluation. Because I have that high level of respect for science, and frankly awe at times, I am sharing my thoughts and admittedly lack of intellectual and practical patience for what has and is continuing to occur as of this writing from the Trump administration. Mining the information presented by the president I have found only a rare occurrence of truth but more often what is discovered are exaggerations and errors, and "playing down"[11] information not openly communicated to the public. I am a member of the elderly cohort that is viewed as susceptible to potentially becoming part of a troubling and growing number of American cases and deaths, along with those globally, who test positive for the novel coronavirus (Covid-19).[12] The true facts are important to everyone, not the politicized banter of the Trump administration playing with lives.

Covid-19 is rarely out of the minds of people around the globe. Each of us, as the data shows, can unknowingly be a carrier of the virus and not present symptoms. And yes, anyone can fall victim to the Covid-19. There is a difference to being aware and responsible versus a hypochondriacal outlook. Yet the Trump cancer finds it difficult to accept the scope of the pandemic but instead is looking for some type of personal victory to assure his reelection.

Controlled efficacy and safety studies are mandatory before broad scale availability of therapeutics or vaccines can be made available to the public. The often repeated "good feeling" voiced by the president about a drug that has been available for years for a totally different indication has unsubstantiated credibility. Leadership for now, it seems, will come from each of us as individuals to take to heart what each of us can do. The guidance and credibility for those steps comes from researchers, epidemiologists, clinicians and all those on the front lines of management, *i.e.*, medical providers at every level.

If after reading this book some feel that what I have assembled is only some sort of partisan indictment of the president that is truly unfortunate. The preponderance of evidence accumulated about the Trump cancer and its administration is difficult to ignore. The behaviors of the sort exhibited by this president, and his own words, are quite enough to indict anyone, regardless of political affiliation. As someone who served several rewarding years as a professor in a respected journalism school, I steadfastly taught my students that research, objectivity, fact-gathering and a commitment to sound ethical behavior must lead in their work. Some will say that what I've written is not objective at all. For those in that camp I suggest that they compile emotion-free, fact-based evidence and then reach their own conclusions. Opinion is indeed personal, and I am distressed by what I observe and hear daily from the Trump administration, his enablers and those who would rather just look the other way.

So, am I guilty of what some would describe as editorializing in this book? I represent but one voice, but to blindly accept the Trump cancer rhetoric does not bode well for any of us. Do I encourage others to dig deep for facts and science? Absolutely. Do I hope that this book will deliver information that can help others more thoroughly consider what is happening to the country and to each of them? Certainly. Changing anyone's mind about their views of the management being undertaken by the Trump administration to address the Covid-19 pandemic as an example is only a realization and outcome each person comes to for themselves. In another non-fiction book I authored[13] I stated that I was not telling anyone what to think. Rather, I wanted to provide information for readers to think about and could provide knowledge and perspective through which to arrive at their own informed opinion. I believe I have successfully held to that same objective here.

What has and is happening to America today is not pretty or acceptable. The Trump cancer is indeed unchecked, shocking and dangerous to our collective future. Incompetence and lies do not build confidence nor facilitate intelligent progress. How can lies possibly be viewed as being "aspirational" or said differently, who would want to aspire to success based on being a highly skilled liar? Well, apparently the Trump cancer can as it seeks recognition as a martyr. A true martyr sacrifices something of value and even life itself for the sake of a principle. Trump, on the other hand, believes his martyrdom is a certainty by sacrificing nothing but American lives and threats to our democracy, with principles not even placed on the table.

Our future is being coerced, not led, by Trump. His lack of skill and aptitude are combined with those in place around him who seem to be motivated to only stroke his ego and compliment his every word. This blind subjective strategy positions the country's future outlook on a very shaky footing, if not on many levels placing it in jeopardy. In their own way his staff and supporters are helping to facilitate the cancer spread. There is little to be positively confident about from constantly shouting at rallies, capitalized tweeted threats or attacks directed toward individuals and mismanagement of the country's institutions. Any reliance on Trump is a commodity offering little assurance. We are all capable of understanding what is happening to us and responsibly we can always search for truth. Each of us can contribute to the well-being of the patient, our country. That mental orientation is essential. Our calculated participation in seeking truth is tantamount for achieving a meaningful and successful future. The

Trump cancer's impact on the country is devastating in many ways and treatment must be built on hope, faith in our democracy, trust in government responses and unwavering leadership demanded by Americans. Eradicating the Trump cancer and its almost maniacal quest for power is a necessary first step in a regimen of care and health for the country.

In arriving at an opinion about the importance of character as a human attribute the 19th century orator Robert Ingersoll offered the following. "Nearly all men can stand adversity, but if you want to test a man's character, give him power." Character is not something that you buy, steal or manipulate into being. It is the sum of one's experiences, actions and behaviors that are cumulative over a lifetime of learning. But a strong character built on one's abilities and history can be lost very quickly, and once lost is difficult if not impossible to regain again. Power properly applied can be used effectively but it can also degrade reasonable and responsible behavior. If flaws in character accompany an assumption of power, there are opportunities for having a deceptive first-person orientation to the world, having an expectation of entitlements and all manner of guidance and rule are left aside with corrupt consequences.

Trump was given a level of power at his election that exceeded anything he had ever known or perhaps had even conceived possible. He had operated in his own world of deception and corruption for decades with lofty expectations but with little regard for the opinions of others. His character had been questioned along the way, as well as his business practices, ethics and morals. In a sense he may have felt that prior to the presidency that he was destined to be viewed as an elite businessman, bon vivant, entrepreneur and superior to all those around him. He may well have thought, or even aspired, to be viewed as a martyr outside of his own mind, but most assuredly he had ignored the wisdom of Mahatma Gandhi who said, "let no one lust for martyrdom."

In a medical environment when an individual receives a cancer diagnosis there are basic questions that are surfaced, the answers to which provide both guidance and instruction. What kind of cancer do

I have? Where in my body is it located? Will it spread? Is it treatable? What are my treatment options? What might I experience during treatment? Certainly there are more questions that can be asked, but consider these few in the context of a Trump cancer diagnosis. The type of cancer and its location touches every aspect of our lives. Treatment can take root in both the legislative and judicial branches of government and outcomes for the country can address both near- and long-term possibilities. Most notably, Americans can prevent a recurrence of the disease.

The presidency has placed the Trump cancer under the microscope. Each cell affected is an American. Trump is examined about his political behavior and world leaders are scrutinizing his slow erosion of the US position in the world. His actions evoke a negative assessment of his ability to lead or make meaningful contributions that do not reflect his egotistical approach to most everything he touches or desires. His ability to react in knowledgeable and favorable ways to concurrent and unanticipated crises forces investigation, not just observation. The Trump cancer's place in history is assured, but not in a way he can control, and not necessarily complimentary or following a pathway to martyrdom. What's that phrase? Oh yes, be careful what you wish for…sometimes you fail.

"A lot of damage has been done to our fragile republic.
Repairing that damage won't take months or even years.
It will take decades, if not generations, to pull our
deeply divided nation together again…
We now find ourselves on the precipice of a great cliff.
Our next step is either into the abyss or toward a higher
moral ground. It's up to you, my dear friends.[14]

CHAPTER ONE

Cancer is Not a Trustworthy Malady

"He who does not trust enough will not be trusted."

LAO TZU

In a medical application the term malady is used to describe, and occasionally in a generic fashion, a condition in the human body that is potentially resistant to determining an accurate differential diagnosis and an effective treatment regimen. Routinely this presents a challenging and unwelcome scenario for both healthcare providers and patients. Beyond the impact on one's physical body the detrimental effects of a medical malady on the mind and one's emotional stability can be devastating. Treatment for such a condition requires a gathering of experience, diagnosis parameters to be established and investigated, and a coordination of the combined knowledge, skills, energy and dedication of many.

The suffering cancer patient, no matter the stage of their disease, is in the hands of medical professionals, and frequently researchers,

1

to call on all historic and investigational resources to arrive at a resolution for treatment. The objective is always to provide care and interventions toward achieving a remission of devastating destruction in the body and enervating the control of the disease characteristics toward finding a cure. Above all, no matter how uncomfortable decisions may be that must be made, trust is required. A successful finale demands it. Without unhampered trust included in the treatment regimen indecision can frequently occur. Valuable time will be lost, and the defiant malady will continue to wreak havoc on the body, precipitating further deterioration while the patient voices an accompaniment in the form of a cacophony of cries for help.

Cancer is not trustworthy. Cancer is manipulative. Cancer cares nothing about the host, caregivers or healthcare providers. Cancer does not look to share positives, only negatives. Cancer does not accept, it denies. Cancer is described in stages of disease but cancer the villain could care less. It emphatically seeks control. Cancer assures and seeks to cause damage. Cancer is only interested in itself and surviving in ways that benefits itself.

The cancerous Trump presidency is indeed a malady of similar description, making its impact in a fashion similar to cancer threatening the body, and the suffering patient in Trump's case is the country. And, the country is indeed crying for help. It is offensive to the mind and the senses to be both an observer and a victim as Trump corruptly and indiscriminately winds his way through all facets of American lives. It has been widely established that trust is not a concept that the president willfully applies to others. He expects trust, and loyalty, only to himself. His lies and false claims do not generate trust in anyone. Trump is not unique as he embroils himself in controversy, with no limitations, no filters of any kind and with little regard for the negative impact of his behaviors on people or the country. As of July 9, 2020, Trump had made 20,055 false or misleading claims in 1,267 days in office.[15] Those numbers are alarming and assuredly will increase. As of that date the president of the US has made over 15 false or misleading claims each day, and yet scores of Americans hang on his every word. A further look at the data also shows that from the early months of the pandemic and moving closer to the November 3, 2020 election, the number per day is even greater.

What is so utterly unbelievable is that Trump makes no effort to encourage trust toward himself or in his debilitating approach to the presidency. He prides himself on bragging about his gut instincts; forget the knowledge and the experience of others to help guide him. If these admirable characteristics found in others are averse to his opinion those individuals are "wrong." Why, because he says so. It just doesn't seem to matter to him to be trustworthy or to acknowledge or exhibit all of the positive accoutrements that being trusted could provide. There are those who outwardly invite the disorder he initiates and are equally unconcerned that facts must indeed matter. Outrageous statements that provide neither substance nor facts provide the reinforcement that the Trump cancer demands. Trumps wants to be in charge and expects to be worshiped in his mutation of Dali Lama intellect, or as he as voiced it in another way, "I am the chosen one."[16] Shortly after making this incredulous self-righteous reference it was reinforced by outgoing Energy Secretary Rick Perry.[17] Some speculated that Perry's comments were a quite obvious an attempt to substantiate an "imperfect Christian man" and endear Trump to evangelicals. But perhaps it should be recalled that during the primary season leading up to Trump's eventual nomination for president by the Republican Party, Perry had referred to Trump as a "cancer on conservatism."[18] Perhaps joining the president's Cabinet made him a convert.

The "the chosen one" descriptor from Trump's mouth was viewed as an attempt at making a religious declaration and connection with a particular block of voters but nevertheless raises questions with Americans, including about trust, because of a lack of credibility associated with his previous religious statements. Americans overall don't think Trump is particularly religious: A majority say Trump is "not too" (23%) or "not at all" (40%) religious, while 28% say he's "somewhat" religious and only 7% say he's "very religious," according to a Pew Research Center survey.[19] What these findings mean in terms of impact on his possible reelection are not clear, but for many a trust in a higher power has great meaning and Trump demonstrates over and over that the higher power he promotes himself. The Bible speaks to things the Lord detests, and among these are a proud look, lying tongue, a false witness who speaks lies and sowing discord among brethren.[20] It would be an interesting discussion indeed if Trump were to lead a small group Bible study.

The Trump cancer is extraordinarily apparent in the president's tap-dancing role as president, but not as a stalwart of responsible leadership as he woefully attempts to appear knowledgeable in addressing a crisis such as the Covid-19 pandemic. Trust is lacking in so many ways. One must try to understand the president's motivation for not acting with any degree of appropriateness based on his lack of acceptance of advice and knowledge from those most qualified to provide guidance. Time after time as experienced governmental leaders, both state and federal, clinicians and epidemiologists have provided information upon which actions to manage the pandemic can be intelligently based, the president often ignores the counsel, put his own twist on that information or makes statements that are not factual. His word choices are incorrect, and always exaggerated, but certainly successful in making him the center of attention. He doesn't seem to recognize when it would be a good idea to stop talking, he and continues to make statements that contribute to confusion and contradiction of the experts. The boy just can't help his gaslighting tendencies. No matter his desire to be all-controlling, he instead is the personification of a spoiled petulant child.

Whoever tries to imagine perfection
reveals his own emptiness.

———————— GEORGE ORWELL ————————

Empty, an apt description for the Trump cancer's abilities and the antithesis of a perfect situation requiring trust. Perfection is the persona that Trump prefers to portray about his intellect, behavior, insights, actions, etc., but frankly it is just an unattainable goal. At the time of the impeachment hearings in the House Trump continually attempted to tout his perfect call with the Ukraine. First there was a memo from the White House summarizing the call, but not a true transcript of the conversation. Then there were the endless denials of a *quid pro quo*[21] with the president of Ukraine on the call by the president and members of his inner circle, a true cancerous situation at work. There were reputable firsthand witnesses to the call who testified to the inaccuracies of the memo summary that was first issued as well as later when a "transcript" was provided by the White House. A transcript requires a source from which an accurate word for word documentation can take place, *e.g.*, a skilled court stenographer or an actual tape recording. There was no stenographer or recording to provide that documentation, only notes from White House staff. It would be interesting if there were ever an opportunity to compare these notes in an unaltered fashion. Were the notetakers in the room actually writing down the same things? Testimony given before the House Intelligence Committee indicated that reality from witness testimony and notes were far apart. And there was that move in the White House where documents concerning this call were filed away on "a secret server." The cancer was growing, and any semblance of trust was deteriorating, but not for the Republican majority in the Senate or the Trump cancer's base of supporters. Like any loyal group Trump's base consists of individuals who are responsible and construct their opinions on their own knowledge and research and have history of responsible voting. There are others who might be described as followers, caught up in the enthusiasm of the moment and a forthcoming election. Missing, perhaps, is an understanding that the president does not have absolute power and there are consequences even for that individual. There are also subsets of these components that make up the Trump base, but the Party to which Trump and his supporters claim allegiance is no longer the grand Republican Party of old nor reflective of its conservative principles. The Party has markedly changed under Trump and elected Republicans live in fear of opposing Trump rhetoric and actions.

The presidential cancer exerts control through Trump's desire to always be seen as the expert, just name the topic. His ability to lie is so very easy for him. Most often there is no logic to his statements or how he so adeptly connects one thing to another in his brain. Without any self-control he pushes out words, some repetitively in the same sentence, and most frequently a convoluted jumbled syntax of false information results. His lies have no boundaries and quite literally they don't remain within the borders of the US. They circle the globe in quick fashion and then the reports of those statements he characterizes as fake news, regardless of the documented fact that the statements reported are his own. Hopefully the hardcore members of his base of support will understand that he is lying to them as well. No one is immune to this cancer but ostensibly many actually welcome it.

Trump is not a hero nor will he ever join that otherwise well-deserved assemblage of humble human beings. It's Americans who are bonding together to fight the pandemic, medical providers, first responders, governors and local officials who recognize needs and the steps needed to fulfill them and the business community coming together to address long-standing issues in our society. It should not take the death of a family member or friend from Covid-19 to motivate mitigation compliance. Trump's empty assurances that ignore both data and expertise far beyond his capacity to comprehend are quickly followed by sarcasm, winks and distasteful and blatant damaging accusations towards others. The effort being applied to the pandemic by true professionals do not deserve the shameful and in no way proper remarks coming from the Oval Office. Commander-in-chief? In title only. "Thanks to the president for his leadership" is a mantra frequently heard, but other than the vice president looking for a way to perhaps remaining in Trump's good graces for the next election ticket, the leadership statement is at best described as a throw-away line of protocol, something that is expected to be said rather than something believed.

> *Remember not only to say the right thing in the right place,*
> *but far more difficult still, to leave unsaid the wrong thing*
> *at the tempting moment.*

——————— BENJAMIN FRANKLIN ———————

Franklin had it right. His counsel above does not just focus on words chosen. He is also addressing self-control and introspection before declaring opinion. The Trump cancer is a perfect example of the lack of both, words and self-control. A limited vocabulary combined with little to no organization of thought is a recipe for disastrous commentary on any topic. The motivation to express oneself in the first person, but occasionally in third person as well, drives Trump to constantly be reaching for something to say that he feels is important, even though that is indeed quite a reach. Read a verbatim transcript of most any speech when he goes off prompter and topic, or answers to any question by a member of the press, or a one-on-one interview. The compulsions are obvious as are things Trump speaks in "the tempting moment."

The compulsion of the Trump cancer is the absolute need, want, and desire that everyone should bow to and accept the thoughts and expectations of the Trump way. His narcissism is not unlike that of a dictator who has this same sort of mentality and will quickly work against those who do not sublimate themselves to his edicts. The substance of Trump's expectations is centered around himself. To imply, above all, that he has the interests of others at heart is nearly comical to consider. The only valid way of existing in the Trump world is to not disagree with him, not criticize him, or in any way have a belief that an idea one may have may actually be valid, innovative, provide an alternative yet contributory view and may actually complement a Trump decree, or wish. To hear the president say that he will make a decision based on his instinct as he points to his head is a scary proposition.

Consider, for a moment how, from the beginning of his presidency, and not inconceivably during his life prior to entering the political arena, the Trump cancer has grown but not necessarily to the benefit of the anyone but himself. Think about it. This man has never taken a battery of psychological tests before being hired. His father didn't require them. He has never interviewed for a job with an HR professional. He may have "interviewed" at the feet of his father, but perhaps not. He proclaimed himself the best candidate for president from the beginning. How could he be wrong about that? There was no vetting of his suitably by his Party, only the primary debates where he showed his lack of respect for the other candidates in demeaning ways and in spite of the superior qualifications of many of those opponents, Republican voters felt Trump was the answer to their prayers. During the period of the campaign the prevailing opinion, and most likely even understood by Trump himself, was that he wouldn't win the election. It was another show business moment for Trump when he won, and the Party had to grin and bear it. But then, the bad dream turned into a nightmare as the country learned of his missing suitability for president as he droned on about crowd size at his inauguration, his continuing nasty remarks about his opposition candidate, and most everything else long after the election was over. Being generous panic will have that effect, I suppose, and talking about what you think you know will delay and disguise the deficits that would soon surface in his presidency. Rewind: that strategy is far too generous and defies any evidence that Trump cared about perceptions as he was just defending his greatness.

Over and over again Trump installed individuals in his administration to positions of authority, or so they thought, only to find that most any interaction with Trump could be a career-limiting move after a relatively short tenure in the Trump realm. Many found themselves looking in from the outside because they had the audacity to disagree with Trump or in some manner worked in responsible ways but not necessarily in the Trump way. It's not unlike an occasion when a medication is given to treat a disease but later is found to be rejected by the body or it does not provide the desired efficacious outcome. The Trump cancer is in a perpetual rejection mode. Trump has selected individuals to work with him, for him, that it appears he felt he could control. Said differently, do his bidding. The back of their business cards must read, "don't think and remember you signed a non-disclosure agreement." Some have bowed to Trump's controlling nature. Others have found that their character, ethics and intellect are not compatible with the "my way or the highway" commands from the president, his rules if you will. To their credit, many have gladly taken the high road.

Control. Control. Control. Observing the president in any situation where he must extemporaneously answer questions truthfully, particularly from the media, Trump will interrupt before the question is completed. The cancer is omnipotent. He may not like the question directed to him or on numerous occasions dislikes a particular reporter or media outlet; he does hold grudges. He will often provide a comment that does not answer the perceived question he thought was coming his way, or more likely will go off on a tangent that provides him the opportunity to bluster in an almost histrionic fashion about whatever is crossing his mind at that moment and includes the songs (deflections) from his greatest hits album. He instructs the media questioner to "write this down" and frequently berates the individual as if that once again demonstrates his authority and quest for authoritarian control over the media.

Even in situations where he might responsibly defer to an expert in the room, he will return to the microphone and exercise his need to have the last word, and then twist or even contradict the far more informed comment that had just been delivered. This occurs even when that other individual's remarks were accurate and reassuring for the public. Control. It is as if he is saying how could anyone not totally agree with my opinion? Almost predictably he will show his disapproval with sarcasm and anger, striking out at individuals even when they are trying to help him but the interpretation in his mind must be that "they are telling everyone that I'm wrong." Rather than acknowledge the opinion of others, even when constructive advice is given, the control gene kicks into play. It is certain that Trump would never describe himself as controlling but quite obviously he is, or severely wants to be. He would eagerly give a discourse on how open he is even when all evidence from those around him, including those who have left the administration and have spoken candidly, are decidedly not in agreement with that position.

Trump's controlling nature also feeds his narcissism, his preferred pathway to his opinion of himself and his abilities, while at the same time creating a self-barrier (wall?) between those who he perceives would like to take control away from him on some level. He doesn't trust and increasingly he demonstrates that he is not trustworthy. The manner in which he attempted to control information about the Covid-19 pandemic threat was coming from a position of creating the image that he knew more than anyone else. As he downplayed information contrary to his genius, what was soon to become evident was that his statements were not only false but dangerous to the country and Americans. Trusting in the government, and in particular the president, is as important now as it was in the administration of President George Washington. Washington was well aware that the United States was a fledging independent nation and as such trust in the newly founded government was essential. Communication in the late 19th century both in frequency and delivery was not what we take for granted today and thus it was even more important that Americans trusted its leaders. The concept of transparency was not in vogue as it is today but that need was indeed what was behind the leadership style of our first president.

"Ninety-nine percent of failures come from people who make excuses."

———————— GEORGE WASHINGTON ————————

Trump has routinely blamed the Obama administration for most anything that is brought into question regarding his administration's response, or lack of, to areas of national importance. At the point Trump signed an Executive Order regarding police brutality following protests around the country in May-June 2020, he stated, "President Obama and Vice President Biden never even tried to fix this during their eight-year period. The reason they didn't try is because they had no idea how to do it."[22] It evaded Trump that the events were occurring during his presidency. This tweet is yet another misrepresentation of reality. As one example, Obama, following a highly visible police-initiated shooting in Ferguson, MO in 2014, instituted several initiatives including the limitation of local police departments having military gear and developing court approved consent decrees providing direction for reforms. By the way, Trump has rolled back some of these positive steps.

Trump repeatedly has stated that they (the Obama administration) never thought something like the pandemic would ever occur and that necessary resources were not available. "But they also gave us empty cupboards. The cupboard was bare. You've heard the expression, 'the cupboard was bare.' So, we took over a stockpile with a cupboard that was bare."[23] This is another convenient lapse of memory about information that Trump had been provided but may have not grabbed his attention at the time. The national stockpile was not empty, but the scope of the coronavirus pandemic was far larger than could have been authoritatively anticipated. Trump was once again setting himself up to be a hero of sorts when in fact the statements he was making were conveniently incomplete and false.

From a public health and crisis implementation standpoint, Trump and his team were provided considerable information that was not acted upon. But given the opportunity to deflect blame for doing nothing in the early weeks of the Covid-19 pandemic, the Trump cancer is quick to jump through any open door to distract from its failures. On more than one occasion briefings that were supplied to Trump prior to his inauguration and since have gone ignored or at least not been given the attention that they deserved. Important to understand in view of the Covid-19 pandemic is a report developed in 2016 by the prior National Security Council (NSC), *the Playbook for Early Response to High-Consequence Emerging Infectious Disease Threats and Biological Incidents.* The Trump administration was briefed on the report in 2017. The report was apparently only deemed important by some but never acted upon.

Although the lack of cooperation between the Trump-controlled transition team was remarkable, recall that New Jersey Governor Chris Christi had been replaced early on by the vice president-elect. Trump had to have control. Sound management and rule of law be damned. But the Obama administration tried to soldier on to make things as seamless as possible if only for information sake and its commitment to Americans. There was not much more the predecessor could do to fight off the Trump cancer.

Case in point: The Trump administration was made aware of the need for addressing the potential of a pandemic situation in a briefing from the prior administration before his inauguration. On January 13, 2017 in its waning days the Obama administration set up a transition exercise on the topic of pandemic preparedness. The purpose of the exercise was to discuss different scenarios in the face of a pandemic so that Trump's team would understand how policies and practices would apply. Trump officials were told that pandemics can begin in other countries and find their way to the US as borders do not matter and science at multiple levels provide critical guidance. What is so very interesting now in 2020 is that the conclusions[24] of the exercise, if embraced by the Trump administration at the time, may have changed outcomes early on in facing the Covid-19 pandemic timely actions can make a significant difference. These conclusions included:

- Science and the characteristics of the disease should drive response decisions
- Early recognition of a situation dictates the importance of timing.
- A unified national response and messaging are critical
- Medical countermeasure strategy is key for success," including social distancing and addressing shortages in ventilators and personal protective equipment.

Two-thirds of the Trump representatives in that room during this pandemic exercise are no longer serving in the administration. The White House news release on January 14[25] did not specifically identify pandemic preparedness as one of the topics of the exercise but did provide a list of attendees. Keep in mind that this was a transition exercise in 2017 and three plus years later only Steven Mnuchin, Mike Pompeo, Wilbur Ross, Betsy DeVos, Dr. Ben Carson, Elaine Chao, Stephen Miller and Marc Short remain as members of the Trump administration and some not currently in the positions in which they were initially appointed..

Attendees missing from the administration today through resignations, firings or nominees not confirmed, and one awaiting criminal sentencing, included Reince Priebus, Rex Tillerson, General James Mattis, Representative Ryan Zinke, Senator Jeff Sessions, Senator Dan Coats, Andrew Puzder, Dr. Tom Price, Governor Rick Perry, Dr. David Shulkin, General John Kelly, Representative Mick Mulvaney, Linda McMahon, Sean Spicer, Joe Hagin, Joshua Pitcock, Tom Bossert, KT McFarland, General Michael Flynn, Gary Cohn, Katie Walsh and Rick Dearborn.

The Trump cancer has an obvious aversion to science and scientific innovation. These things are too hard for him to understand particularly when he makes no effort, yet as hard as Trump may try, he can't manipulate science. He and his cronies attempt to spin scientific facts and expertise as a plot against the economy. A classic novel from decades ago about a controlled world stated that, "Science is dangerous, we have to keep it most carefully chained and muzzled."[26] Trump would rather talk dollars but even in these instances what he tallies is most often exaggerated and misrepresents a true picture of the expenditure, or income in the case of tariffs and personally.

Another example of Trump and his administration ignoring critical information that could be used to not only affect health strategy development but also planning response implementation in view of a pandemic situation came in the form of an exercise that took place in August 2019. After two plus years in office ,with his people in place in his first term, eliminated the possibility he could place blame for not knowing the exposed needs to manage a potential pandemic. The exercise was called the Crimson Contagion and was focused on a flu pandemic, interestingly that originated in China, and first appeared in Chicago. The exercise involved 19 federal agencies,

12 states, 74 local health departments and 87 hospitals. During the course of the four-day exercise Trump administration NSC officials were briefed.

The report compiled following the exercise contained these conclusions:

- Insufficient federal funding sources existed
- Confusion about the implementation of the Defense Production Act (DPA) was apparent
- Supply chain and production capacity was inadequate
- Global manufacturing could not meet US demand for personal protective equipment and ancillary supplies
- A prediction of 110 million infections, nearly 8 million hospitalizations and 586,000 deaths without a coordinated national response

Thus, four months prior to the first reports of the novel coronavirus Covid-19 in the US in January 2020, the assessment from the Crimson Contagion exercise was evidently not of sufficient importance for the Trump administration to initiate any sort of responsible action during that period. If the cupboard was indeed bare, which it was not, why weren't definitive actions initiated? The majority of the conclusions listed above have come to pass. The toll on human lives is ongoing. The Trump cancer was preoccupied with himself and ignored the long-term public health consequences for Americans. Indefensible.

Although denials have subsequently surfaced, a story reported by ABC News in late November 2019 centered on US intelligence officials warning that a contagion was very apparent in China's Wuhan region. A detailed analysis was included in a report by the National Center for Medical Intelligence (NCMI) indicating alteration of business and health risks to the population was being threatened, according to ABC.[27] The first Covid-19 case in China was reported December 1.

"We assess that the United States and the world will remain vulnerable to the next flu pandemic or large- scale outbreak of a contagious disease that could lead to massive rates of death and disability, severely affect the world economy, strain international resources, and increase calls on the United States for support."[28]

The Trump administration has gone further to ignore preparedness, by not only underfunding these efforts but also by proposing steep spending cuts year after year to institutions, such as the Centers for Disease Control and Prevention (CDC), that are tasked with investigating and handling outbreaks. Congress has resisted these efforts in the bills Trump has ultimately signed, but the president's requests have nevertheless spoken to his priorities. His budget proposal for fiscal year 2021, released in February 2020 when the Covid-19 outbreak had already reached the United States, called for the CDC's overall funding to be slashed by hundreds of millions of dollars."[29] How is it even possible that a sane individual would even consider such a move? Again, it's an aversion to the importance of science and preparedness beyond the pandemic that was upon the world and certainly poised to explode in the US.

The following is a milestone chronology of action/inaction by the cancerous Trump presidency between January and April 2020. The number of pivotal meetings, plans discussed to be undertaken, announcements, missteps, etc., constitutes a far greater listing. Nevertheless, the information points to how delays led by the Trump cancer provided a false sense of trust for some and alarm for others. In the face of an escalating public health crisis the Trump cancer's priorities were not about the well-being of the American people.

January 22, 2020: Question put to Trump: "Are there worries about a pandemic at this point (the first case in the US announced the previous day)?" "No. Not at all. We have it totally under control. Its's one person coming from China and we have it under control."[30] Scientists were already waving red flags about the potential for the virus spreading, including the WHO. *Note*: Fast forwarding to the second week of April, about 11 weeks later since Trump made his "under control" statement, Covid-19 had spread around the world. In the US at the first of July, five months after "it's under control," over

2,911,888 citizens have tested positive for the Covid-19 and over 130,000 have died.

January 28, 2020: An article appeared authored by two former Trump administration officials appeared in the *Wall Street Journal*. "If public health authorities don't interrupt the spread soon, the virus could infect many thousands more around the globe, disrupt air travel, overwhelm heath care systems and worst of all claim more lives."[31]

January 29, 2020: A memo from Peter Navarro[32] circulated inside the White House warned of the pandemic's "potential death toll in the US and estimated the cost as much as much as a $6 trillion."[33]

January 30. 2020: "We have it very well under control,"[34] the Trump cancer boasted. The very same day the World Health Organization (WHO) declared the Covid-19 a public health emergency that required the attention of the international community.[35]

January 31, 2020: Trump calls for a travel "ban" from China.[36, 37] From that point forward he continuously made statements saying his action was taken over the objections of "almost everybody," and he saved thousands of lives in the US. It appears through fact-checking from multiple sources that this was not the case. In reality there were thousands of individuals entering the US after the ban on travel from China. What Trump was not openly acknowledging at the time was that the Covid-19 was already spreading to other countries from China. Further, it was later demonstrated the delay in the US restricting travel from Europe may well have significantly contributed to the spread of Covid-19 in the US particularly as travelers entered through New York area airports. Trump also did not seem to understand that people coming into the country and landing at one of the three New York area airports did not stop there. Many continued travels to destinations elsewhere in the US and early on there were no mandatory quarantine periods established for these travelers.

From this point forward through the end of February the Trump cancer was basically concerned with itself while criticizing others. Essentially there was little in the way of preparing for what was going to be a health crisis situation in the US. Instead, Trump was only concerned with "keeping numbers low" and giving daily evidence that his lack of attention or understanding were indicators of his underperforming as a leader of the country. During January he conducted four campaign rallies around the country (Wisconsin, Iowa, Michigan and New Jersey). In February there were four additional campaign rallies (New Hampshire, Arizona, Colorado and South Carolina), a Super Bowl party at Mar-a-Lago, grand marshal duties at the NASCAR Daytona 500 race and several big-donor campaign fundraising events. All the while, medical experts, scientists and epidemiologists were speaking about the potential for community spread of Covid-19.

The Trump cancer was apparently nervous. So much time was being spent on activities focused on being reelected at the same time that Trump was being distracted by himself and the cancer growth was on the march revealing how little he understood about what was soon going to be enveloping the country and how unimportant communicating truthfully to Americans was on his agenda.

February 2, 2020: Trump stated: "Well, we pretty much shut it down coming from China. We have a tremendous relationship with China, which is a very positive thing. Getting along with China, getting along with Russia, getting along with other countries."[38]

Later the Trump cancer Pacific Rim ping pong match went back and forth from complimenting China's President Xi to accusing the WHO of favoring China and criticizing this proven responsible global organization for making wrong calls. In April he announced he was withdrawing financial support to the WHO. He was touting a similar irrational rationale and using false facts in critiquing and criticizing NATO earlier in his tenure, and then the US withdrawal from the Paris Agreement to combat climate change signed by 197 countries in 2016. In a documentary film on life lessons from Robert McNamara, former Secretary of Defense under President John Kennedy McNamara stated, "If we can't persuade nations with comparable values of the merits of our cause, we'd better re-examine our reasoning." [39] Trump may contradict himself and on occasion rollback one comment to offer another one, but rarely would it be possible to predict that any level of reexamination had occurred. His scattered approach and impulsiveness drive most everything the American people and the world hear from him.

For example, proving his loyalty to no one, even one to which he had momentarily tied his economic designs, his criticism of China increased with a caveat, "Just finished a very good conversation with President Xi of China. Discussed in great detail the CoronaVirus (sic) that is ravaging large parts of our Planet. China has been through much & has developed a strong understanding of the Virus. We are working closely together. Much respect![40] Was his "praise and slap" approach to Xi about the virus or about money (tariffs)?

Trump continued his banter about the "mess" he inherited regarding preparedness for a pandemic. In his animated public statements, he glossed over the facts that didn't suit his administration's lack of attention. His blame deflection regarding an outdated system and tests overlooked the simple fact that prior test protocols (influenza, SARS, MERS, Ebola) were not going to be applicable to this new virus. Science, remember? It's just easier to attack and play the blame game than admit his administration did not heed warnings before and after his inauguration, and in the years since that pandemic preparedness required his attention.

February 7, 2020: The Federal Reserve indicated that the virus could pose a significant threat to economic growth.

February 10, 2020: Trump asserted his theory about the Covid-19 and medical science. "By April, you know, in theory, when it gets a little warmer, it miraculously goes away."[41]

February 13, 2020: Health and Human Services Secretary Alex Azar announced a plan for surveillance in five cities to measure the potential spread of Covid-19 in the US, even though the number of cases at the time was small. It was recognized that having an early indication of a spread in this country was essential. Unfortunately, the ramp up of the surveillance system was not ready in those cities and the tests at the time were not effective because of a component that precipitated inconclusive results. The CDC was not totally on board with the Azar announcement.

February 23, 2020: "There is an increased probability of a full-blown Covid-19 pandemic that could infect as many as 100 million Americans, with a loss of life of as many as 1-2 million people, young and old. Time is of the essence on all four points of the PPE, treatment, vaccine and diagnostics!"[42] A trusted Trump adviser in his administration, Peter Navarro, was sounding the alarm and waving red flags but no one was listening, and Trump was blind to the impending disaster headed straight at his presidency.

February 25, 2020: Two days later Larry Kudlow, the Director of the National Economic Council (NEC) in the Trump administration weighed in with his fantasy opinion on the Covid-19 situation. "We have contained this. I won't say airtight, but pretty close to airtight. We have done a good job in the United States."[43] Another Trump administration science denier.

February 26, 2020: "Because of all we've done, the risk to the American people remains very low," Trump said. "We're ready to adapt and ready to do whatever we have to as the disease spreads, if it spreads. We're very, very ready for this."[44] On this same day Nancy Messonnier, MD director of the National Center for Immunization and Respiratory Diseases for the CDC, stated, "we expect we will see community spread in this country."[45] Trump went ballistic upon learning about her publicly stated opinion.

February 27, 2020: "Now the Democrats are politicizing the coronavirus," he said. "We did one of the great jobs. You say, 'How's President Trump doing?' They go, 'Oh, not good, not good.' They have no clue. They don't have any clue. They cannot even count the votes in Iowa."[46] Interesting turn of a phrase because as the coronavirus pandemic continued to be identified as a serious concern, it appeared that over a period of time, that the Trump cancer "did not have a clue," or at minimum was keeping what Trump did know from Americans.

February 28, 2020: An editorial was published in a prestigious medical journal. "The Covid-19 outbreak is a stark reminder of the ongoing challenge of emerging and reemerging infectious pathogens and the need for constant surveillance, prompt diagnosis, and robust research to understand the basic biology of new organisms and our susceptibilities to them, as well as to develop effective countermeasures."[47]

March 6, 2020: Trump made an appearance at the CDC headquarters in Atlanta and proudly announced that he "understands and gets this stuff." It did not appear that he was particularly concerned that there were over 300 cases of the Covid-19 confirmed at this point and went on to state that "anybody who wants a test will get a test, that's the bottom line." And not one to miss an opportunity to bang his own drum, he made a sudden turn to, "The tests are all perfect, like the letter was perfect, the transcription was perfect, right?" Trump said. "This was not as perfect as that, but pretty good." Yet another cancer deflection from reality.

From the beginning Trump had trouble distinguishing between seasonal influenzas and Covid-19. It seemed they were all alike to him. But as in most things he looked at numbers even though the meaning of statistics evaded him. The data early on in particular, as continuously stated by the clinicians and scientist members on the White House Coronavirus Task Force, and by other administration officials, was most likely understated because of the gaps in reporting of testing and a lack of reporting connectivity between state and local laboratories with the CDC.

During this period, it had become accepted that community spread of the virus was occurring and that mitigation steps undertaken on a broad basis may have a needed positive impact of "flattening the curve" of the spread. These steps included washing hands frequently, using disinfectant sprays, and not shaking hands. It is this last recommendation that Trump chose to demonstrate both his refusal to understand the importance of these relatively simple recommendations and his ("I feel very safe") invincibility; "you can't be a politician and not shake hands,"[48] but later it was reported he said that because of Covid-19 " he wouldn't have to shake hands with these disgusting people."

March 9, 2020: When Trump was visiting the CDC on March 6, he indicated that he didn't know people died from the flu. Subsequently on this date he tweeted: "So last year 37,000 Americans died from the common flu. It averages between 27,000 and 70,000 per year. Nothing is shut down; life & the economy go on. At this moment there are 546 confirmed cases of Covid-19, with 22 deaths. Think about that!"[49] These statements may be the first big reveal of where the Trump cancer was focusing his attention...the economy. He unleashed a barrage of tweets trying to invigorate falling financial markets in view of the economic impact of the virus.

March 11, 2020: Trump blocked most travel from Europe. In spite of Trump's focus on China as the key to halting the spread of the coronavirus, later research indicated that the coronavirus began to circulate in the New York area by mid-February, weeks before the first confirmed case, and that travelers brought in the virus mainly from Europe, not Asia.[50]

March 11, 2020: WHO made its announcement that the Covid-19 outbreak was a pandemic. (US level: 1,267 confirmed cases and 38 deaths; more than double the number of cases Trump stated two days prior).

March 12, 2020: In an effort to appear in control and calm a concerned nation, Trump said, "...we are marshalling the full power of the federal government and the private sector to protect the American people. This is the most aggressive and comprehensive effort to confront a 'foreign virus' in modern history."[51] But in what was an attempt to be seen as reassuring and confident the reaction to the speech while it was being made, and subsequently, was negative. He continued with routine misstatements that required correction later, such as the botched travel ban communication.

March 13, 2020: Trump declared a national emergency,[52] and as he is always wont to do, attempted to further deflect any criticism toward him for his slow response with this tweet: "For decades the

@CDCgov looked at, and studied, its testing system, but did nothing about it. It would always be inadequate and slow for a large-scale pandemic, but a pandemic would never happen, they hoped. President Obama made changes that only complicated things further…"[53] He made no mention of his administration's proposed CDC cuts to people, budgets and programs.

The multiple opportunities that Trump has had to correct all of the shortcomings he has blamed pre-election and since on Obama, and Bush for that matter, just are not important to a cancer that steels itself against factual information. Experts that do not say the things the Trump cancer wants to hear, express sound logic to be applied or proposed appropriate action to be taken are just anxiety producing interferences for Trump. (US level: 1,678 confirmed cases and 41 deaths).

March 15, 2020: Trump acknowledged that the Covid-19 was a "very contagious virus."[54] (US level: 3,536 confirmed cases and 68 deaths). In two days, the number of cases more than doubled and deaths increased by one third.

March 16, 2020: Trump announced federal recommendations for social distancing recommended by the NIH and CDC and no gatherings over 10 people. By this point many state and local governments around the country had already taken steps such as closing schools and limiting social gatherings. Waiting on the Trump cancer to awaken was not an option.

Dr. Anthony Fauci, Director of the National Institute of Allergy and Infectious Diseases, National Institutes of Health (NAID), and a member of the White House Coronavirus Task Force has gone on record stating that "no one is going to deny" that more lives could have been saved during the Covid-19 crisis if the Trump administration had implemented social distancing guidelines prior to March.[55]

March 17, 2020: In a somewhat pathetic attempt to showcase his vast medical knowledge, Trump stated: "This is a pandemic. I felt it was a pandemic long before it was called a pandemic," Trump said at a press conference with the Task Force. All you had to do was look at other countries."[56] (US level: 4,477 confirmed cases and 87 deaths)

Why did he keep his superior intellect about the pandemic hidden? This statement comes from the same person who was surprised that the seasonal flu causes deaths. Trump had begun to use words like battle and war and referenced the coronavirus as the "invisible enemy." On the day the number of confirmed US cases surpassed 6,000 and over 100 deaths he stated, "I view it as a, in a sense, a wartime President. We had the best economy we've ever had. And then, one day, you have to close it down in order to defeat this enemy."[57] The Trump cancer's comments seemed like a desperate search for a place in history as a wartime president, but hardly on a par with many predecessors who had occupied the Oval Office during times of crisis. A change of direction for certain, another distraction and somewhat confrontational, as he continued to refer to Covid-19 as a "Chinese virus" and deflect blame in the direction of his good friend President Xi.

A week earlier he had tweeted, "The Fake News Media and their partner, the Democrat (*sic*) Party, is doing everything within its semi-considerable power (it used to be greater!) to inflame the Covid-19 situation, far beyond what the facts would warrant."[58] The natural understanding ability he had touted at the CDC at the first of the month was apparently lagging behind reality. Trump continued to ignore facts and data in favor of schoolboy attacks.

It appeared the economy was uppermost in Trump's mind, more so than the escalating health crisis, as he repeatedly made references to everything he had done for the country, the stock market, etc., and how he wanted to open up the country quickly. The economy had been strong in prior months and it was the strongest thing he could speak about in terms of his desire for reelection, but he never showed evidence that he could make the distinction between the stock market and the economy. His comments were rooted in campaign rhetoric as he, and other administration officials and most notably the vice president as chair of the Task Force, continued to throw out numbers about testing, test kits available, ventilator production, etc. The focus was on things but not on the people fighting the virus transmission in numerous ways or those treating suffering Americans. The phrase lip service comes to mind.

March 30, 2020: As the Trump administration, and maybe the president himself, began to recognize but not admitting its errors in not taking more definitive action earlier to help the medical community at the state and local level, Trump started making veiled accusations about, in his mind, an exaggerated the need for the volume of protective materials and equipment that were being requested. For example:

"That statement was made, that they have been delivering for years 10,000 to 20,000 masks. Okay. It's a New York hospital. It's packed all the time. How do you go from 10,000 to 20,000 to 300,000? 10,000 to 20,000 masks to 300,000?

"Even though this is different. Something's going on, and you ought to look into it as reporters. Where are the masks going? Are they going out the back door? How do you go from 10,000 to 300,000?

"And we have that in a lot of different places. So, somebody should probably look into that, because I just don't see from a practical standpoint how that's possible to go from that to that.

"And we have that happening in numerous places. Not to that extent. That was the highest number I've heard. That's the highest number you've seen, I would imagine, right? But this man makes them and delivers them to a lot of hospitals. He knows the system better than anybody, and I think you were more surprised than I was when you saw that number, so thank you very much. I hope I didn't get any of your clients in trouble, but it could be that they are in trouble."[59]

There is so much wrong about these statements, and certainly they were not helpful in any way for those in need treating Americans. Medical providers, as well as state and local governments, were looking to the president for help. Workers were being overwhelmed. In spite of their dedication these professionals were becoming mentally and emotionally exhausted in their battle with Covid-19 while seeing the impact on patients, caregivers and their own families as they were concerned about taking the highly transmittable virus to their homes. And the president, well he was making unfounded accusations as if there is some sort of a conspiracy that hospitals and governors must be exercising to hurt him. The good news was and is that the Trump cancer cannot control or destroy the commitment of these people.

Critical thinking is not the forte of the Trump cancer. Rather than any attempt to understand the true answers to the "concerns" expressed and ask reasonable and important questions about how to proceed, the Trump cancer once again attacked those who took exception to his biased yet uninformed opinion. In this case the answers are just not that complicated to discern. The protocols for medical providers facing a contagious outbreak dictated increased safety and treatment measures over and above routine procedures in place for both the containment and treatment of Covid-19 patients.

Of course, the equipment needs were significantly increased because of the growing patient load in hospitals for first responders and others just trying to be safe. Providers were working long hours, exposing themselves to the virus pathogen over and over. They needed protection. They needed to protect those they were interacting with, coworkers and patients. In spite of Trump's lack of understanding, this was not a seasonal influenza. It is a far more contagious situation and not fully understood while research was be redoubled to learn more. Patients were presenting themselves at hospitals, clinics and private practice offices. In each of these settings healthcare workers throughout required protection. Not having the opportunity to change their personal protective equipment (PPE) not only brought a level of risk to patients, but also to the providers themselves. The demand for PPE was not extravagant. It was essential. Changing mask, gowns, gloves, etc. was what was required for ethical medical coverage. The volume of patients, alarmingly illustrated by the growing number of cases, required that protective equipment needed to be worn and changed more often. Everyone in potential contact with those diagnosed and being treated had to comply and as they also faced undiagnosed yet potential carriers of the virus. Those wanting to prepare for a worst-case scenario was not extravagant. It was responsible immediate and crisis management in the moment and what experts were predicting would be required in the future.

April 7. 2020: "The cases really didn't build up for a while, but you have to understand, I'm a cheerleader for this country, I don't want to create havoc and shock and everything else. But ultimately, when I was saying that, I'm also closing it down. I obviously was concerned about it."[60] Watching television for multiple hours each day is not enough, it seems, for the Trump cancer to recognize the havoc it was most definitely creating on many fronts. The wartime president had no strategic plan, just paranoia about the coming election.

April 11, 2020: "I think the situation is unprecedented, and there is no question about that. It's whiplash! The economy was moving forward at a rapid pace in terms of growth, jobs and even wage increases, and all of a sudden, the pandemic hit, and the economy was shuttered. This is unprecedented, it is unsettling and challenging but, we will rise to meet the occasion."[61]

As time passed state governors took responsible steps to manage the crisis far better than any leadership evident from the president. States sourced needed ventilators, medications and personal equipment for medical providers. Businesses and institutions in communities took it upon themselves to help in a variety of ways to support medical providers and first responders. Manufacturers with capabilities to retool kicked in as did sources that were unexpected such as auto racing teams that used their in-house expertise to produces items such as face shields and ventilators. The president sought out some manufacturers to use their factories to help with shortages, but at the same time the states found themselves in a bidding war with the federal government to access these items. Administration officials stated the position that the national stockpile was for the federal government's use and was not to serve as a warehouse for the states. To make it even clearer Trump stated, "It's a stockpile. That's why we call it a stockpile." That was helpful.

In his own strategic thinking example, at one point son-in-law Kushner, a Trump cancer analog, stated, "And the notion of the federal stockpile was it's supposed to be *our* stockpile. It's not supposed to be states' stockpiles that they then use."[62] Realizing the public relations disaster that statement created after media questioning, the HHS revised its website as follows: "Strategic National Stockpile is the nation's largest supply of life-saving pharmaceuticals and medical supplies for use in a public health emergency severe enough to cause local supplies to run out. When state, local, tribal, and territorial responders request federal assistance to support their response efforts, the stockpile ensures that the right medicines and supplies get to those who need them most during an emergency." Ensures is a fairly straightforward and strong directive, but not necessarily well implemented in the early months of combating the coronavirus. During the same period the Trump cancer took the position that even the growing need for tests to not only diagnose but track the virus across the country was not the government's responsibility. "We're not standing on street corners selling tests." The Trump cancer had a sarcastic and valuable retort for any perceived threat to its wisdom.

April 13, 2020: On the occasion of what was supposed to be a briefing about the pandemic on this day, it instead morphed into a remarkable egotistical display of ignorance about the Constitution as Trump returned to his magnificent authority to ignore social distancing and stay at home guidance, and thus reopen the economy. He wanted everyone to believe that his authority superseded any action on the part of the states. "I'm going to put it very simply: the president of the United States has the authority to do what the president has the authority to do, which is very powerful. The president of the United States calls the shots."[63] Authoritarian guidance at its best from the president but not enforceable.

Reading, studying and understanding the Constitution is too much of a leap to think that it might ever have occurred, or its principles had been embraced by Trump. It is quite impossible to know in advance what spectacle the Trump cancer will reveal at any given moment to demonstrate how little he understands about the US system of government. His comprehension of laws and process is lacking and for certain he missed the point about the colonies' independence from a monarchy. Instead, he sees himself with a crown. The 10th Amendment to the Constitution, part of the Bill of Rights and like the Constitution itself developed by the colonies (states), is pretty clear. It's about a division of power between the states and the federal government. "The powers not delegated to the United States by the Constitution, nor prohibited by it to the states, are reserved to the states respectively, or to the people."

April 17, 2020: The WHO reported over 113,000 cases of the Covid-19 spread in more than 100 countries.

The pandemic provided a real time example of why trust in the man and his administration is quite impossible to accept. The only things consistent about the man is his lack of character, obsession for assigning blame for his mistakes to others and his inability to be a president of what was the most respected country in the world. Among the list of targets at which he has directed blame include the WHO, China, Obama, Bush, Democrats, the media, governors, states, hospitals, athletes and multiple agencies. A basis for trust does not exist. The cancerous tendencies adopted by Trump through his inept mismanagement style are played out daily and are dangerous for the country as it fights to maintain morality and not increase mortality.

"We have done things the likes of which has never been seen; no one would have believed possible what we've done; more than any time in history." These repetitive statements are all true, but not in the complimentary manner in which he would like them to be interpreted and accepted. What the cancerous Trump presidency has done is damage and divide the country and incite culture wars and in ways "never before imagined" coming from a president. In the US, citizens can demand trust and civility be restored and assure once again that they find their place in the Oval Office by defeating this cancer on democracy at the ballot box.

"

CHAPTER TWO

Trump's Cancer Doesn't Hide

"When widely followed public figures feel free to say anything,
without any fact-checking, it becomes impossible for a democracy
to think intelligently about big issues."

THOMAS L. FRIEDMAN

It is quite impossible for the Trump cancer to hide. In many ways each day the president throws his cancerous folly wholly on the table for all to see, with the assumption and expectation of acceptance by all. Acceptance of his words, his will, his negativity, his questionable racist statements, his incompetent acts, his rejection of civility and his obfuscation of the rule of law.

The basis for Trump's frequently bizarre statements is incessantly difficult to understand. Logic cannot be applied nor any diagraming of his sentence structure. It is very interesting, some might say pathetic, that the president can be so disconnected with the country at large that in his failing attempt to be a leader and achieve a martyrdom legacy he consistently, and perhaps with his greatest skill quite adeptly, makes things up as he goes along. To be fair, making things up may be what he does best, but certainly this is not helpful, most always inappropriate and certainly not acceptable. He assaults women with his words. People of color are assaulted with his words. Democrats in general are assaulted with his words. Those who don't agree with him are assaulted with his words. He even assaults his base with words and actions, but they don't see it, or maybe they just accept the behavior. Using a very small repertoire of words and topics, the vile cancerous statements become jumbled examples of attempts to appear intelligent and presidential, but this is quite an unachievable objective for Trump. On more than one occasion he makes light of critical commentaries that raise his lack of presidential competence. He is embarrassing on the world stage, even mocked by leaders of democratic countries around the globe, with a few exceptions whose motives are not always clear when complimenting the "leader of the free world."

Journalists, wherever their country of origin, work to provide the country and the world for that matter, with facts that inform about the president's actions, his interactions with Congress, his personal war with data and his dismissal of evidence-based information. Any analysis of what the president might be trying to achieve for the country more often concludes with questions about is it about the country's needs or is it what will satisfy his most burning need, i.e., unchallenged power and personal greed. The form that journalist communications take, from print publications and broadcast, to usage of the Internet and technology in many ways, all combine to routinely provide both answers and questions about the Trump administration. The discrepancy in coverage between Fox and Friends, a Rush Limbaugh radio diatribe and other conservative entities is most remarkable compared to any and all news outlets and public policy organizations that lead with confirmed facts rather than sensational and inciteful jargon. Trump perceives that unless a media source of information is clearly conservative in its orientation that all others are out to interfere and criticize him with "fake news." But having blinders on does indeed make him blind to the country's needs as a whole. Trump reacts egotistically to criticism in any form. Trump cannot stand still and be shown he is wrong even if different thoughts and positions could actually be helpful to him in some way. His id makes him blind to that possibility. Trump must also have loyalty from all around him at all costs. He shows his lack of trust by requiring signatures from those around him on what he thinks are forever binding non-disclosure agreements. Cancer's loyalty is parochial too. Like cancer that believes only in itself, the cancerous Trump disease too is loyal as well, but only to himself. It just can't be any other way. Cancer doesn't care about who it invades or who it hurts along the way, and neither does the Trump form of this disease.

News story topics have incredibly varied focus on the Trump cancer but sourcing evidence for these reports is relatively easy to identify, primarily as the early guidance of paths to pursue are readily identified by the cancer itself. Trump just can't help it. The Trump cancer is not lurking in a hidden fashion as cancer in the body often does. A cancer in the body can appear at any time, sometimes early in its attack on body systems and organs, but often it appears at a later stage after the scourge has developed to a point that any combination of surgery, chemotherapy and radiation is more an offer of hope for patients and families and a prayer for a favorable outcome. The Trump cancer has demonstrated that it is not fearful of criticizing former presidents nor concerned with learning from those whose governing experience is a benefit, not a curse. Becoming familiar with history and policies, foreign relations, diplomacy, and understanding the importance of intelligence briefings is critical and the wealth of information expansive. Unfortunately, none of these things seem to appear on the Trump note cards.

Trump sees no need or value to take advantage of multiple opportunities to expand his knowledge and form a responsible basis for decisions through reading, study and listening to those whose careers have been focused in multiple areas of essential wisdom, including governing. The President's Club, as it is known, is a repository of knowledge from its members. The current living presidents and their civil ongoing relationships even with differing partisan views remain willing to continue to serve the country and the current president when asked. Trump, as a woefully unprepared president, sees no value in consulting his predecessors as his knowledge is supreme…just ask him. What he is willing to do is criticize all of them, Republican or Democrat. He would take it as a sign of weakness consulting past presidents and exposing such a move to his base. Living presidents today, with some notably more vocal than others, are embarrassed by the current occupant of the Oval Office. First ladies too have insights that cut through the noise and clutter of adversarial and attacking expressions. Michelle Obama startled the nation with her insightful and simple recognition and directive statement. "When they go low, we go high."[64] Those few words say so much but are never to be understood or incorporated by Trump. Knocking down locker room doors with locker room bravado and expletives is more the Trump style, i.e., going low and then still lower. More recently Ms. Obama went further to illustrate the lack of ability of Trump to be president. He famously stated during an interview about US deaths from Covid-19, "it is what it is."[65] Ms. Obama took his own words and used them to describe the "cold hard truth" about his presidency. "He simply cannot be who we need him to be for us, it is what it is."[66]

A recent simple, but sincere gesture from a former president in the face of a growing public health crisis suggested that partisanship be put aside. Differences are very small in comparison.

"We are not partisan combatants. We're human beings, equally vulnerable and equally wonderful in the sight of God. We rise or fall together. And we're determined to rise." [67]

In typical fashion, at a time when what could have been used as a bonding moment for the country, was instead turned into yet another opportunity for the Trump cancer to raise its ugly head. Rather than at least acknowledge a former president's suggestion for making progress, Trump responded:

"Oh bye(*sic*) the way, I appreciate the message from former President Bush, but where was he during Impeachment calling for putting partisanship aside." @foxandfriends He was nowhere to be found in speaking up against the greatest Hoax in American history![68]

Missed the point entirely. No hiding. No reason. No purpose. The Trump cancer says, "it's about me."

The Trump cancer begs for attention yet with great frequency when attention is received this cancer resorts to a favorite back-patting response, "the likes of which has never been seen before," or some equally tired variation of it such as, "I am greeted with a hostile press the likes of which no president has ever seen."[69] These types of absolute statements are a Trump trademark. They range from the self-spoken adulation he thrives on and directs toward himself, to a preponderance of claims that frequently are related to his "oh poor me" role in life as "the biggest victim the world has ever seen." In the latter instance it is as if he cannot fathom the possibility that he is not as omnipotent that he believes himself to be with thoughts pervading his personal assessment comparable to: "Why don't be people see how great I am?" "Why don't people love me?" "I am always right, and I am the only one who can fix it." It is admirable for anyone to project self-confidence, but this is not what is being displayed. For all the world to see at any time his statements rarely, if ever, demonstrate an association with truth and facts. These basic tenets of leadership just don't seem to matter to him and likely would not even be recognized if laid in front of him. This is because he is only "leading" himself to his warped perception of greatness, power and authoritarian rule. On the other hand, it could also just be that the physiological relationship between his brain's synapses and neurons connectivity just don't exist.

Shying away from the truth seems to be the default position until such time as it may be recognized as a political necessity, or at minimum his ego requires that he must attempt to cozy up to the reality of truth, but by no means in a complete and factual manner. For the Trump cancer these moments may come as his unrestrained anxiety increases from falling approval numbers, or he is caught in denials that are blatantly incorrect or when previous genius statements are shown to be false and fly in the face of documented evidence to the contrary. Invariably the fake news arrow falls rapidly from the Trump cancer quiver as the president strives to somehow reassure himself that he has been victimized when more to the point his own rhetoric has betrayed him. But attacking others is always the fallback position and the outcome that evolves shows that the Trump cancer is invariably struggling for yet another deflection.

The Trump cancer defies and resists the expertise of others as it repeatedly brings the spotlight to itself, outwardly unafraid to criticize others to cover its own mistakes. Out in the open at every opportunity, the Trump cancer is uninhibited. The breadth of topics Trump chooses to address with his proud all-knowing intellect is quite remarkable, particularly when those around him with far more knowledge and insight are routinely ignored, dismissed and contradicted. The "I wasn't told" card is excessively used as an excuse as this cancer's means of deflecting questioning about prior knowledge of a situation. But "that dog won't hunt" as Trump demonstrated very early in office that he didn't read intelligence agency briefing material, did not pay attention in meetings and has been reported by staffers as "being all over the place" with questions that are generally off topic. Because this cancer can't and won't hide, it proudly proliferates its toxicity unrepressed. The Trump cancer believes in itself and the benefits it believes it can create for itself without the impairments of actually seeking relevant knowledge.

For cancers in the body such as melanoma or breast cancer, discovery of the sentinel node[70] is an important diagnostic procedure to follow, not only for immediate assessment but also for use as a benchmark for future diagnostic evaluation and treatment. Knowing when and where cancer cells may proliferate is invaluable information for medical providers. Case in point: The Trump cancer's sentinel node for the progressive cancer stemming from the presidency and pervading the country is Trump himself. It is difficult to predict just where this cancer may go next. Being both the host and protagonist for his cancerous approach to the highest office in the land, and the billboard for uninformed and highly inflammatory statements, this cancer marches through and over the lives of Americans and the global community. Superficial is an apt descriptor of his attitude, every word he speaks, or tweets, and all rooted in a disdain for individuals, institutions, opponents, elected officials and even those he has nominated for positions or appointed along the way. It doesn't seem to matter that the country is structured around the conclusions of the founding fathers and their critical thinking to address the tyranny from which they sought independence, and to provide the framework for order as outlined in the Constitution. "We the people" are not just words on the parchment on which they reside. These words clearly communicate that the country's citizens joined together and carefully crafted the Articles that follow.

"We the people in Order to form a more perfect Union, establish Justice, insure domestic Tranquility, provide for the common defence, promote the general Welfare and secure the Blessings of Liberty to ourselves and our Posterity, do ordain and establish this Constitution for the United States of America."[71]

What matters most to Trump is using the presidency, the bully pulpit, to continue the delivery of boastful and inaccurate misrepresentation of facts and he creates division in the country as a result. Providing unity for the people is not an objective actively pursued by Trump. In fact, unity is only a word he may use but with no intention, plan or ability to make it a reality. His boasts misrepresent situations with great consistency. For example, He brags that he moved the capital of Israel to Jerusalem. Well, not exactly, Mr. President. The US embassy was moved to Jerusalem and the US will recognize Jerusalem as the capital. This might appear to be an insignificant point but not really. He also has stated that the reaction to the move was greater among evangelicals than Jewish people.[72] Quite an obvious political statement in the guise of foreign policy but in addition offensive in large major to many while demonstrating that even small details evade him. While those inside the administration and others outside the administration are doing their best to provide acceptable and factual information to the public, the Trump cancer is oblivious. While it is hoped that some degree of balance and order would result by opposing the Trump cancer's ignorance and resistance to learning, Trump is a continual moving target shifting rapidly from one misstep to the next and certainly with no apologies noted.

The life-altering Covid-19 pandemic faced by the United States and the world for an undeterminable length of time has provided Trump with yet another way to misrepresent facts as it has become the latest "chum in the water" he uses as a distraction from other issues springing from the White House. Even with opportunities to reassure the country in Task Force briefings about Covid-19 illustrated that sentences that began with "we" quickly morphed to "I" as attention is always most tolerable for him when he embarrassingly sings his own praises. The Trump cancer demands to be at center stage, a headlining principal player, but by no means a cast member contributing to a greater performance. During one update briefing a legitimate question asked by an experienced and respected reporter was not answered and instead turned into a Trump tirade. It was hardly a nasty question and a reasonable person would have shown some empathy for Americans and their concerns by answering it directly. The Trump cancer front and center missed yet another opportunity to speak to Americans and in this small way unite the country.

This is but one example of the Trump cancer visibly at work during a dramatically escalating health pandemic, taking the occasion to once again attack a media professional instead of seizing an opportunity to demonstrate leadership. Telling the public to stay calm, openly encourage Americans to follow their medical and local authority directives, embrace the scientific research underway for understanding more about the virus and the efforts to develop therapeutic treatments and eventually an effective vaccine. Only a small degree of compassion and knowledge was all that was required. But for the record the empathy, compassion and knowledge descriptors are not demonstrated by the president on most any topic or situation at any time. Instead his assertions about the coronavirus show a deep understanding and level of concern. "It's a life, it's got a life, and we're putting out that life, cause that's a bad life that we're talking about."[73] The Trump cancer reality approaches the bizarre, is generally uneducated and most certainly dangerous.

Trying to be the smartest person in the room is never going to be a potential accomplishment and in fact is markedly unachievable by Trump. But there are those who hang on his every word as truth and his is the perceived most important opinion albeit missing true and accurate knowledge. As the seriousness of the Covid-19 pandemic was escalating Trump repetitively showed he had little understanding about how drugs are actually developed and studied for human use. It is patently inconceivable that someone in his administration, the White House Covid-19 Task Force, the CDC or the Food and Drug Administration (FDA) had not tried to force his understanding of the process and the time required. Undoubtedly, they tried, but like most subjects where others possess far more knowledge their attempts were most likely admonished. The Trump cancer's pre-presidency history tactically included accepting that throwing money at a problem, ideally someone else's money, as the best solution for most anything, particularly when it benefited him. But he must have cut that business course at Wharton that covered the validity that a point will inevitably be reached when money is indeed not a solution. Yet combine this strategy with the neediness of Trump's personality, and cleverly thinking that making something happen fast makes him look even greater than he feels, scientific research and safety be damned. In medicine this sort of thinking is a dangerous recipe leading to terrible outcomes. Personal history demonstrated that the Trump cancer's genius was not infallible. He experienced numerous instances in his business endeavors where he may have learned that speed and money were indeed not the answer.

Trump has taken the term "fast-tracking" to mean he is correct and moving slow is the antithesis of that, meaning he could not accept being viewed as incorrect. Once again in the evolving pandemic crisis he had sufficient and frequently updated information to be dangerous, far more than dangerous, as he twisted facts into Trump-speak. Developing new medications in an accelerated manner does not supersede the need for responsible evaluation following a phased research process for the investigation of new therapeutic, or vaccine or medical device. Without a doubt the process of establishing clinical protocols, enrolling patients, following the guidance realized from placebo-controlled, double-blind studies to establish efficacy and safety are critical for medical providers and ultimately patients. This must have been explained to him by others, but did he listen? Clinical trials make the difference between an FDA approval for a drug based on evidence, not whim, gut feelings or instinct or show business antics. Evidently Trump's need to be out front, always visible and authoritative supersedes all else. His genius "feeling" was that the professionals must be wrong, because of course he never is. But lest it be forgotten of course, there wasn't a long line of citizens waiting to be injected with bleach that was an approach that Trump felt was worthy of investigation "based on something he heard."

To provide a focal point for direction and communications as the Covid-19 pandemic escalated, the president formed, or someone told him to form, a Task Force to be led by the Trump administration cancer-in-waiting Vice President Mike Pence. If one were to follow the chronology of statements by Pence over a period of days, weeks and months it is obvious, he has adapted well to a Trump cancerous mind-meld in the best traditions of Star Trek[74] movies and Mr. Spock. The information conveyed by Pence in briefings, particularly with regard to any topics around timing, and elements required for managing the crisis had several continuous endpoints. He rattled off considerable political jargon, lots of numbers (had to be in the millions), no specific dates of availability for anything, no evidence of an organized supply chain or distribution plan that medical providers and the public could follow, and of course multiple complementary mentions of the president. What was conspicuously absent was a presentation of a testing plan, a description of how tests were being manufactured, how they were to be distributed around the country and subsequently analyzed, or how the Trump cancer promise of "anyone who wants a test will get a test" would be fulfilled, etc. Pence's comments could have been a tape-recorded loop that could have been played at each briefing, contributing little information and provided little credibility, insights or hope for the country delivered by a suspected android personality. The briefing content began to take on the appearance of a déjà vu experience, much like the movie theme portrayed in Groundhog Day,[75] repetitive and head-scratching. Thank God there were professional scientists and researchers included as members of the Task Force to inject substance into this failed leadership equation and who routinely strived for accuracy and balance in the information presented about the spread, mitigation steps and truthfulness about the potential development of therapeutics and vaccines.

With Pence designated the leader of the Task Force one would have expected that the briefings were his to lead, with deferrals to scientific members and public health officials to supplement the information and answer specific media questions. For a period, this was the protocol with the occasional Trump interruption if he saw an opportunity to try to appear presidential and in charge. And then it happened; not a surprise really, given Trump's need to be in the limelight at all times and certainly not hiding in the wings. The order of things changed for the briefings as the Trump cancer took over. He sashayed to the front of the podium each day and proceeded to present his version of the facts from the lectern. Most often they weren't facts at all but rather his words served as an opportunity to compliment himself and Pence and all others who did his bidding, many of whom collectively had lost their spines. The exceptions were the true professional members of the Task Force, with knowledge and perspective about what was ahead to combat a pandemic that Trump had done little to recognize for what it was, much less develop a plan to overcome it. As the Trump cancer pranced in its personal pasture of lies, defiance of science and impossible to follow pontifications answering media questions that only made sense to him, other Task Force members on the podium featured stares of disbelief, expressions that disregarded loyalty and instead communicated a desire to run for the exit. It had to be an altogether painful experience for them.

Day after day the commentary was the same, but it didn't matter. The Trump cancer was making itself known as it had commandeered the microphone and the briefings took the form of a show and a political event. Trying hard to be recognized as the savior of the country to bolster his reelection prospects, the Trump cancer comments brought up all of the ballyhoo of the 2016 campaign and his condescending album of favorite hits: the outrageous comments he became known for while chastising people and institutions, bragging about his power and his intelligence, degrading those opposed to his positions, presenting his version of prior statements that were clear walk-backs if not coverups, and more. As the days passed media representatives present for the Task Force briefings became fewer as their reason for attending was for information of importance to the nation to convey to the public, not politics. Major broadcast networks would cut away from the briefings until their monitoring of the proceedings revealed that someone was at the lectern actually delivering real information about the country's handling of the pandemic. But frequently as if on cue Trump would return to the microphone and contradict what true experts had just said. On each occasion the Trump cancer showed that it had no grasp at all of the critical scientific parameters that were required to address the pandemic from multiple perspectives. If the reasons for the briefings weren't so very serious this highly obvious Trump act would have been unnecessary. But it was necessary. The country was in trouble and the horizon under Trump was covered in clouds. The country expected a federal management plan of action and instead received political messages, hand-offs to the states and then interference as governors tried to get a handle on managing the problem in their states. However, once again Trump played politics, pitting Republican governors and mayors against Democrats in these same roles.

The outcome from the Covid-19 pandemic is yet to be known, certainly at this writing, but the sorely lacking leadership and misguided opinions from the president will surely be the topic of historians for years to come. It is also worth recognizing that Pence has fully adopted the bob and weave mentality of the Trump cancer when direct questions are put to him. He begins a response on point but then wonders through multiple Trump-eques talking points off the topic, with facial gestures of great sincerity but that do more to communicate "if I just keep talking maybe they'll leave me alone." In spite of the importance of testing and tracing to learn and begin a level of containment of the virus, the many promises of test availability were never realized. Even at this writing there are not enough tests available to test every American, labs doing the analysis have limited capacity, turnaround time for arriving at a test conclusion is predominantly long because of the lab capacity reality and the conclusion of a test, positive or negative, is of questionable value unless the analysis is completed within 48 hours from the time the patient was administered the test. But the Trump cancer has continued to have little understanding, preaches the miracle of the coronavirus magically disappearing, making gross generalization statements regarding resistance and recovery from the virus in children to encourage school reopenings—with little regard for the impact reopenings will have on parents, teachers and staffs and transmission of the virus to them—and an almost embarrassing lack of understanding of the growing volume of data documenting the numbers of positive cases and deaths, particularly in light of the early "economic reopening" of business around the country, and the subsequent resurgence of the coronavirus in many states. The Trump cancer sticks with its own "science" and when presented with facts tells Americans and the world, "it is what it is" as some form of comfort in the face of the pandemic.

Pulitzer Prize winning reporter Bob Woodward made a profound statement years ago that is relevant in any discussion about the Trump presidency, now or in the future. "The central dilemma in journalism is that you don't know what you don't know. I suspect there have been a number of conspiracies that never were described or leaked out. But I suspect none of the magnitude and sweep of Watergate."[76] As out in the open the Trump cancer presents itself is it possible to be certain the full extent of what the country is now experiencing under such a weak president? Woodward may need to reconsider his conclusion that the Watergate conspiracy would not be exceeded in scope or damage. However, for journalists and the country at large, we still "don't know what we don't know," as there are far too many lies that have been spoken to the universe and that the dam will break soon, and the waters of information will flow unimpeded.

During the time of the House impeachment inquiry, regarding Trump's infamous "*quid pro quo* moment" in a telephone call with the president of the Ukraine, Volodymyr Zelensky, Trump was quite outspoken and characterized the impeachment inquiry process as a hoax (of course) fostered by the Democrats. There was indeed much that the House Judiciary Committee wanted to learn, undoubtedly outmatched by the information that the Trump cancer did not want to reveal. During the inquiry subpoenas were issued to: Secretary of State Mike Pompeo seeking a full transcript of the telephone call with Zelensky, personal attorney Rudy Giuliani who apparently was instrumental in the discussion of brokering a Ukraine investigation of former Vice President Joe Biden and his son Hunter because of the president's suggestion in public that this should occur, White House Chief of Staff Mick Mulvaney requesting all White House documents related to the Zelensky call, Secretary of Defense Mark Esper seeking information on any delay of the delivery of $400 million in aid to the Ukraine, and the Office of Management and Budget for any documents relating to a delay in forwarding the aid. Not only did the Trump administration stonewall any type of forthright response to the subpoenas, but Trump also blocked additional multiple witness testimonies. The Trump cancer does not hesitate to be the center of attention but in areas of potential damaging information, *e.g.*, tax returns, private conversations with Putin and yes, the Zelensky call, Trump pulls out all the stops to keep things hidden. What else don't we know? What does the Trump cancer not want revealed?

Congressman John Dingell, Jr., a champion for oversight during his 29 terms helped to expand healthcare in this country, was a strong supporter of the Civil Rights Act, chairman of the Energy and Commerce Committee but perhaps his strongest position came as chairman of the subcommittee on oversight and investigations. From his earliest days in Washington he supported oversight of the executive branch. In his book published shortly before his death he made a final and loud plea for Congress to use all tools at its disposal in conducting oversight of the Trump administration. "I'm told by my young friends that when you write something in all capital letters, you're yelling so, let me shout this out: WE HAVE ABDICATED OUR CONSTITUTIONAL SYSTEM OF CHECKS AND BALANCES IN THE UNITED STATES! Understand this: I'm not saying this as a partisan. I'm talking about anybody in any administration, Republican or Democrat, who thinks they're above the law."[14]

If there is one consistency that has been in play throughout the Trump presidency it is that questioning of anything directly related to Trump or his actions, result in a rebellion against all oversight by Congress. The Trump cancer's irate railings when his decisions are put in question by Congressional committees have a common theme...fake news, hoax and the Democrats. The Trump cancer rebels at any attempt of oversight by Congress. He is so lacking in an understanding of the roles of the three branches of government that instead he has focused how to attempt to manipulate them to his personal advantage in some way. The Constitution does not specifically speak to congressional investigations and oversight per se, but the authority to conduct investigations is implied since Congress possesses "all legislative powers."[77] Congressional investigations are beneficial in helping legislators make more informed decisions about policy, and these investigations contribute in significant ways to the system of checks and balances. The Trump cancer uses all means available to abuse this system and, in the process, corrupt many facets of the US rule of law. When oversight investigations are stonewalled by the president the merry-go-round spins again and again. A case in point during the impeachment inquiry came in a District Court for the District of Columbia decision in the Committee on the Judiciary v. McGahn[78] case, that stated that the White House could not continue its obstruction of Congress. The ruling stated, that McGahn must testify, declaring that "presidents are not kings" and "no one is above the law.[79]

At the time House Speaker Nancy Pelosi issued the following statement. "The Courts have been clear: The President's insistence that he is above the law is an offense to our Constitution and to every American. Today's District Court decision in the McGahn case is yet another resounding ruling that the Administration's claim of 'absolute immunity' from Congress's subpoenas has no basis in the law or our democracy and must immediately cease. Again and again, the Courts have reaffirmed the Congress's constitutional authority to conduct oversight on behalf of the American people."[80] The District Court decision was appealed, of course, and later the ruling was to vacate the District Court ruling requiring McGahn to comply with the House's subpoena to testify before Congress. At that time Speaker Pelosi commented, "Today's split Court of Appeals ruling in the McGahn case does not contradict what the Courts have continued to rule: that the President's claims of 'absolute immunity' from Congress's subpoenas are false."[81]

At one point during the impeachment hearings legal scholars testified before the committee and although there were different perspectives presented, there was considerable agreement between the four, including the scholar requested by the Republican members. This individual, Jonathan Turley, a law professor from George Washington University, was critical of the inquiry process and its timing and called the short timeline for the inquiry "both problematic and puzzling…a facially incomplete and inadequate record in order to impeach a president." He went on to point out that information gaps existed because of "unsubpoenaed (sic) witnesses with material evidence and it is wrong to move forward without hearing from them."[82] This position was welcomed by the Republican members of the committee as wrestling with refusals to testify in the courts would go on for months and most likely until after the 2020 election. That point alone in reality mattered little because once articles of impeachment reached the Senate for trial the Republican majority was certain to acquit the president. Countering Turley's position one of other the scholars, Michael Gerhardt, a professor of law at the University of North Carolina, stated, "The full-scale obstruction of those subpoenas, I think, torpedoes separation of powers. And, therefore, your only recourse is to, in a sense, protect your institutional prerogatives, and that would include impeachment."[83] Gerhardt also stated in his testimony that "I want to stress that if what we're talking about today is not impeachable, then nothing is impeachable." The scholarly arguments presented were indeed educational and pertinent, and in the periods of their testimonies somewhat overpowered partisan politics.

The Trump cancer has had multiple "opportunities" to demonstrate his expertise in managing a crisis situation, those that have occurred on his watch from sources over which he didn't control, as well as those that in effect he has created for himself, and for the country, like his impeachment. Crisis management requires foresight, planning, communications and action. These criteria are not evident at all from Trump or his cronies. A crisis audit is a basic step that takes place far in advance of an actual event occurring and it has been clearly established that even before he took office Trump was advised regarding a possible pandemic and needs to be addressed immediately, not waiting until a pandemic occurred. Do we have the right people in place? Have we established what functions of government need to be represented on the crisis team? Have we researched the situation, and things that have occurred in the past that provide both guidance and an action plan that can be adapted? In the Trump administration it has been shown that the above questions were not answered nor even considered in advance of a crisis such as the coronavirus pandemic occurring. Prior data, action steps and outcomes had not been on his radar at all, and when it comes to communication Trump himself is the worst possible spokesperson for gathering expertise together to address the pandemic with his predictable behavior of paying little attention to their counsel. Of even greater significance, politicizing a crisis like the coronavirus pandemic is an absurd place to start but of course that is exactly where Trump began. What he did most assuredly with his id leading the way was saying and doing things that over time showed his ineptness as a leader, including withholding information from the public, destroyed faith in the current government's management of the crisis and set in place a long-term timeline for recovery that would last for years.

The Trump cancer wants very much to hide but it cannot. Its superficial approach to the presidency is outweighed by its need for adulation. Trump is his own worst enemy and he does not allow himself the possibility of recognizing that. He cannot admit a mistake in judgement or action, or heaven forbid a defeat of any kind, because that admission is a sign of weakness to him as opposed to demonstrating that as a leader, he must candidly own his mistake. The closer truths come to being revealed the more entrenched he becomes and desperately creates more attempts to distract. At some point he will race to a claim of fake, hoax or fraud as the reason for any defeat. Trump chooses to make every problem easily resolved as he presents his simplistic solution of the moment. It is really all he has to offer. But wait for it, the next day the solution will be different coupled with components consisting of lies, undocumented or just incorrect information, a sprinkling of threats toward those who may disagree but decidedly simplistic for certain. There is that long-used phrase "you can run but you can't hide," but in Trump's case he doesn't run and he doesn't hide but demonstrably he stumbles on in full view and accepts no responsibility. There is no real depth of understanding, a willingness to learn or even the smallest possibility that he could speak to any situation with restraint or accountability.

"It is wrong and immoral to seek to escape
the consequences of one's acts."

———————— MAHATMA GANDHI ————————

CHAPTER THREE

A Cancerous Attack on Truth

"A man dies when he refuses to stand up for that which is right.
A man dies when he refuses to stand up for justice.
A man dies when he refuses to take a stand for that which is
true. "[84]

REV. MARTIN LUTHER KING, JR.

Truth. A guidepost for civility, cooperation and progress. As Dr. King stated over 50 years ago not standing up for what is right and just is essential or the character of a man dies.

To the dismay of the American people. and the world, it is really quite simple. Trump does not seek truth. He doesn't care about the truth. He is unconcerned who is hurt by his proclivity for truth avoidance. Truth evades Trump, consistently, as he has braced himself so long against it that it is no longer recognizable, even if he had an epiphany one day and wanted to speak truthfully. But as is seen each and every day, he has no interest in being truthful. Name the topic.

He only cares about what he thinks and then says, true or not. This isn't new behavior as it represents how he has most probably lived his entire life. Becoming president was not a facilitating factor for a sudden behavior change. Trump mirrors cancer in the body as it too only cares about itself but cancer in the body doesn't lie. It's very real and only its progression is not fully predictable.

In Trump's case his single most important pursuit on all occasions is focusing on what benefits him, but certainly not the country. He brought this attitude to the presidency and he has embellished his personal form of a devastating invasive cancer daily. It is not as if he is attempting to disguise truth in the form of a lie. Not at all. It is more a matter of just unashamedly having no interest in making truth a priority as president.

In the pure healthcare sense, the progress that has been made in the diagnosis and treatment of many types of cancer, specific tumor types, and attacks on the body's immune system has been remarkable in recent years. The use of chemotherapy "cocktails" (drugs administered in specific combinations and dosage regimens) as well as targeted therapies[85] have improved positive patient outcomes and survival rates. In particular, coordinated research efforts from governmental agencies, pharmaceutical and biotech companies, using the expertise of renowned oncology research scientists and clinical investigators, have produced advances that would have been impossible to predict in years past.

The statements above pertain predominantly to the life-threatening cancers that the world's population experiences each day. Yet with all of the medical innovations, the word cancer evokes fear and apprehension. It remains a frightening diagnosis for the young and old alike. Parents, relatives and caregivers are closely attached to the diagnosis, perhaps even at a level much higher than other illnesses. Dying becomes top of mind for many and their own mortality is brought front and center.

One major difference today is that unlike in the past people are not afraid to talk about a cancer diagnosis. The "big C" was formally the short-hand reference to cancer without saying the word. Today, patients and families have access to information through technology to become more informed in their understanding about what is being faced and how they can become more involved in their own treatment. Supporters of the Trump cancer also have credible and accurate information access, but research indicates that social media, with all of its errors and bias, continues to have overwhelming influence with these individuals. Fact-checking is sorely missing from tweets and other forms of post using social media. The Trump cancerous presidency is irreparably linked to Twitter® as it continues to metastasize rapidly over many subjects. Lacking evidence that might support the majority of tweets, Trump provides commentary on its own foreign policy, domestic spending, immigration, taxes, administration staff and cabinet turnover. He espouses false representations, blocks legislation prepared by the Democrats, lies on most any topic, supports his inexperienced and unqualified appointees to critical government positions as well as campaign staff and friends sentenced to prison, and even attacking members of his own Party and candidates seeking election. His relationship with most anyone is fleeting if they find themselves on his wrong side. "The president doesn't fire people; he just tortures them until they are willing to quit."[86]

Trump's ascension to the presidency was remarkable by most all accounts. His past was legendary, and not necessarily complementary but certainly all good in the way Trump chooses to recall it. But for many, Trump's presence was incredulous as now he was the leading representative of the Republican Party and supposedly its long-held conservative principles. What Republicans did not consider was how in a very short period Trump himself was going to become a distraction, an embarrassment and a problem, not unlike a cancer that invades a person's body and creates issues across the body's systems and organs. The Trump cancer is slowly destroying the fabric of the country with missteps about things he hasn't bothered to learn about and decidedly that means most every area of governing. Cancer in the human body gains a foothold by invading cells and slowly spreads unless an intervention slows its progress or defeats it entirely. The division Trump continues to create has spread in a similar fashion. In spite of his propensity to misspeak, mis-tweet, lie and point blame, the support from his base remains intact, feeding the cancer and encouraging it to continue its behaviors. The importance and recognition of truth escapes many while the Trump cancer continues to flourish.

"Truth is incontrovertible, ignorance can deride it, panic may resent it,
malice may destroy it, but there it is."

—————— WINSTON CHURCHILL ——————

There are certain truisms about cancer and its deleterious impact on patients and families. Likewise, there are truths about the characteristics and demeanor of Trump, and many in his ever-changing administration, that are at best, continuously negative influences. As hard as he, his staff, his appointees and his family members try to walk away from it, truth will prevail, and they all will eventually be caught up in the fallout of discovery. The country has become increasingly divided and the Trump cancer has shown resistance to all manner of reason and the necessity for truth. Boisterous speeches, incoherent thoughts, blatant lies and an obvious overuse of the first-person personal pronoun demonstrates the narcissistic avoidance of truth as a tenet of Trump as president. Other opinions are unimportant. Military experts are ignored. The intelligence community is undermined. By ignoring facts and authorities who can help shape reality through informed and understood actions, Trump only knows enough to have a treacherous impact. Regardless, he does not hesitate to attack people, policies and the rule of law at every turn. The only "truth" he acknowledges is what passes the lips of the president.

It is from this perspective that the danger from Trump pronouncements and actions surfaces some sort of problem nearly every day. There seems to be a personal prevailing attitude that if he thinks something, on most any subject, it must be real and, in his mind, true. His inner circle of advisers seemingly have a lack of influence on him, if they even still try, if only to simply tell him that neither his limited knowledge nor his desire to be right all the time combine to work in the way he wants. Verified evidence doesn't get in his way as he rarely uses specifics to vocalize his opinions. If he does recall something that he heard from some source it is not at all unusual for him to misstate the information, embellish it and in many, many cases just twist it just the way he needs to make it fit his political agenda. To assume that in every case there was an authoritative source for every statement he may make would be a tragic mistake.

The trust the nation needs to have in its president is compromised in exceedingly disturbing ways by the Trump cancer, with consequences that affect the country through misuse and abuse of the branches of government for his personal, not presidential, advantage. Just as cancer in the human body routinely compromises organs and systems, the Trump cancer mirrors that effect in many ways on the country. Nothing is sacred. His claims form the basis of quick and rash statements that by design or accident confuse and/or deflect true responses to relevant inquiries. It is impossible to take Trump seriously as even in what may seem to be small inconsequential matters truth is not important to him. Truth builds trust and if the small things are constructed around lies, where's the potential for trust of the president on any matter that has far reaching effects for Americans and global relationships? As Mark Twain wrote, "Lies can travel halfway around the world while the truth is putting on its shoes." It's clear that the Trump cancer walks barefoot all the time, every day.

"If you don't tell the truth about yourself,
you cannot tell it about other people."

—————————————— VIRGINIA WOOLF ——————————————

For many individuals, cancer takes away hope and their power to fight, resist and overcome. These common consequences take root with the long-standing belief that a cancer diagnosis is a death sentence. Trump too has taken away hope for many, but citizens have retained their power to advocate and generate change. In the body cancer creates its own shield against change, i.e., a welcome remission for the patient. It can lurk in the shadows of the body, not be discovered until late stages or be concealed in other areas not originally detected. The Trump cancer by comparison is easily detected, widespread and devastatingly consequential.

The Trump cancer is proud of its malignant impact and it enjoys spreading its chaos. This cancer is thrown in the face of the Americans every single day and is frighteningly out of control. The Trump cancer doesn't hide because its host believes there is no one on the planet who is more capable, intelligent, or insurmountable in his ability to fix all. The words routinely used by this host to describe itself, and to criticize those who wish to rid the country of his destructive behaviors, are most often incoherent, repetitive, insulting, uninformed and even laughable if it weren't for the grievous downside impact they generate.

Cancer in the body is the ultimate truth-sayer. It has no allies as it depends on itself, for both resistance and growth. It feeds itself. It turns the body against itself. Cells that are destroyed deteriorate organs and systems that weaken the body. The Trump cancer has done the same to the country. Trumps allies in government, and perhaps that is too strong of a term, are made up of those who are more minions, blindly obeying his wishes. They are contributors to the dysfunction and the destruction left in their path. But why, in face of the predominate and consistent examples of Trump making demands from an egotistical point of view, do his supporters remain unchanged? Is truth not important? The Trump cancer too seeks its own rewards as in human form cares only about itself. Ego does drive Trump as he spreads a proliferative cancer throughout the government but with a questionable lack of attention to true benefits for Americans.

The Trump cancer focus on numbers whatever the category, whatever can be misrepresented, whatever can be lied about in a way that in some bizarre sense supports his disjointed agenda of fear and loathing for anyone who doesn't support him. He uses numbers to provide fodder for tweeting and media attacks but routinely with a fair degree of exaggeration and/or misrepresentation of their true meaning. Money is his primary motivation, not the well-being of Americans, and it is as if every member of his base of supporters understands that they are not necessarily "profiting" from all the things he is shouting at them. Information must be sought, not just force-fed with Trump's sugar-coated bias that disguises facts. He is quick to take credit for the economy, positive unemployment figures, etc., but what is not known are the actual contributions that he personally has made, beyond threats and dismissing staff and experts along the way. Further, he misrepresents the data in gross ways to present a picture that is favorable to him, and yet with just a modicum of research it is quite easy to show that what he says is not true. Unemployment figures and new jobs are monumental examples of massaging the numbers. The repetitive Trump cancer SNAFU's,[87] to use the decades-old military term, are quite visible representations of the malignancy of this presidency.

National security are not the only words that he truly does not understand, nor does he have a real plan to achieve this state, but the words are used only as part of rally rhetoric to gin up his base and defend his disjointed immigration "policy," or is it White House senior advisor Stephen Miller's? Miller has consistently been on the side of controversial topics such as white nationalism, immigration and minorities, and viewpoints some would describe as on the fringe at the time. In an article in *Los Angeles Magazine* a high school classmate recalled a statement Miller made when questioned about a classroom incident when the instructor was focused on the meaning of patriotism and using the American flag as a prop. His classmate recalls when Miller was asked why he didn't see the instructor's example as a teaching lesson and Miller reportedly responded, "The truth doesn't matter; it's about what people want to hear."[88] If Miller has carried this opinion with him through the years, it may explain his apparent simpatico relationship with the Trump cancer. Miller's statement about the truth not mattering could be the Trump's replacement of President Harry Truman's desk plaque, "the buck stops here." Fortunately for the country during his tenure, President Truman's plaque was about presidential accountability.

The Trump cancer disguises truth and destroys hope. Instead Trump creates false hope by continuing to misrepresent true facts and creating his own "facts" as he attempts to sound authoritative, and directed to all who want to believe him for whatever their reasons. There is quite an astounding awareness that Trump only surrounds himself with individuals who won't disagree with him. He sheds both experience and knowledge and instead rewards bigotry, racism, nepotism and totally biased politics above all else. This is the only effective "wall" he has built as he uses the circumstances of his staff saying "say whatever he wants" as a barrier to the truth. He eliminates people by one method or another and demands loyalty. The Trump cancer threatens all who won't follow his costumed direction as he plays the role of president for his own benefit, shrouded in the makeup of accusations and inaccurate soliloquies. The result is that the cancer grows uninhibited. For those who do not have the interest or initiative to seek legitimate information, this cancer habitually fools them into support based on few facts, and makes them willing players in this show business, fallacy presidency. They stand and applaud as the coercion from the Trump cancer invades their very being.

The truth seems to have never found a welcoming home with this president. It appears to be so unimportant that recognition of truth vs. manipulative attacks appears to be quite impossible for him. The dark clouds of division precipitated by denunciations of anyone with alternative views to his childish musings are not based on truthful reflections or critical thinking in any form. He is only critical of others, but not the result of introspective evaluation of his positions, as disturbing as they be. But consider that for a moment. It is not unusual for presidents to be criticized as anyone can experience moments when they might be a target for some form of criticism, but every single day in multiple ways?

During his impeachment hearings in the House he made the focus, from his Twitter forum, on a "transcript" of his now infamous call with the Ukraine president. His comments about the call that he repeatedly described as perfect was a memorandum summary of the call became controversial as this document varied significantly with the opinions of others in the room at the time who testified before the House committee. This and other material were then stored on a "secret" computer server. The entire matter brings back a line from the movie "Animal House"[89] when Dean Wormer revealed that the subject disreputable fraternity was on "super-secret probation." But the fraternity didn't know that, and the public may never know what the secret server cold reveal. The cancerous processes in the Trump White House meets this description pretty well. Consider the various other things the Trump cancer has hidden from view, *e.g.* tax records, preventing staff to testify in House impeachment inquiry.

Trump's statements and missing leadership surrounding the novel Covid-19 pandemic is another perfect example of his winning at all costs philosophy without employing truth. In this case Trump has repeatedly established that he doesn't understand the science, doesn't appreciate the science in terms of how the virus presents itself, or how scientific principles are followed for investigation of the potential spread of the pandemic, drug investigation, etc. He contradicts scientific authority with a passion second only to his lust for money. The Trump cancer only has respect (patience) for what it says and unfortunately feels compelled to share a variety of those inner thoughts with the world. His attempts at communication about Covid-19 most often result in a disjointed repetition of words through both his Twitter diatribes and his live statements. Without fail he demonstrates that his thoughts are random. He is in effect talking to himself and he likes what he hears. But because of the peculiar positions he does make public one can only imagine what he may be thinking that never surfaces. Official statements ostensibly suspected as frequently being choreographed by a friendly news network are followed with Trump statements, tweets or answers to media questions in the occasional press briefing or in gaggle settings as he leaves the White House for Marine One.

The cancer reveals itself handily when at the beginning of any response Trump identifies the question topic, but in short order branches off into an endless variety of unrelated subjects, disconnected thoughts, rants, accusations and more, that most often have little, if any, bearing on the question that was asked. This stream of consciousness "communication" style does very little to fulfill the information needs of the public, particularly on something as critical as a health pandemic. In preparing a true transcription of either the Trump cancer's opening statements at a briefing or a response to a media question one would find it to be a frustrating use of time for those seeking information. In the first example he reads from some sort of a prepared statement written by others or bullet points organized for him. But rather than follow the hoped logical order he lands on a word and then editorializes, most often to turn the point political, self- aggrandizing or critical of someone or something. Answering a media question follows the same haphazard approach, but generally is even worse and with great frequency insults the reporter, criticizes his or her media outlet and the quality of the question.

The questions that follow were addressed to the president at a recent White House briefing about the country's response to the pandemic, and the verbatim responses illustrate the difficulty in receiving valid and structured responses from the president most anytime.[90]

Question: "Are you considering an executive order to basically ban the export of medical equipment?"

Response: "I don't know that we'll need that, but I think it's happening by itself. I think a lot of things are happening. Well, some people -- we make the best medical equipment in the world, and you have some people like the European Union, they don't take it, because they have specifications that don't allow our equipment in because it's designed in a different way.

"Even though it's a better way, it's designed. They're all -- they're all playing games against us, okay? They've been playing games against us for years, and no President has ever done anything about it. But the European Union -- if you look at medical equipment, we make the best medical equipment in the world, but we can't sell it because -- or not appropriately."

"And yet, we take their medical equipment in our country. We're changing things, Steve. All of this is changing. But they have specifications so that our equipment -- designed specifically so that our equipment can't come into their countries. It's a very terrible thing that's happened to our country.

"And, let me tell you, some of the people that took the biggest advantage of us: our allies. You know, we talk about allies. They took advantage of us in many ways, but financially as well as even militarily when you look at -- Look, I got -- if you look at NATO, the abuse that was given to our country on NATO, where they wouldn't pay, and we were paying for everybody.

"We were paying -- now, because of me, they're paying a lot. Now they've paid a 125, 135 million -- billion dollars more. And then, ultimately, Secretary General Stoltenberg -- who, I think, you would say is maybe my biggest fan -- we got them to pay an additional $400 billion -- billion -- other countries.

"And -- but -- but you know that. And then there's the trade. They make it -- they make it almost impossible for us to have a fair deal. They know this. They know I'm just waiting. We have all the advantages, by the way. It's going to be easy when I decide to do it. But this isn't the right time to do it. But we've been treated very, very unfairly by the European Union."

Question: "Sir, lawmakers and economists on both sides of the aisle have said that reopening the country by Easter is not a good idea. What is that plan based on?"

Response: "Just so you understand -- are you ready? I think there are certain people that would like it not to open so quickly. I think there are certain people that would like it to do financially poorly because they think that would be very good as far as defeating me at the polls. And I don't know if that's so, but I do think it's so that a lot of -- that there are people in your profession that would like that to happen."

Follow-Up: "But your own medical experts did not endorse that plan yesterday."

Response: "I think it's very clear -- I think it's very clear that there are people in your profession that write fake news. You do. She does. There are people in your profession that write fake news.

They would love to see me, for whatever reason -- because we've done one hell of a job. Nobody has done the job that we've done. And it's lucky that you have this group here, right now, for this problem, or you wouldn't even have a country left. Okay. Go ahead, in the back, please."

The last question concerning Trump's desire to "open the country by Easter" was, at minimum, troubling. Rather than a clear response as to how that proclamation wish could be accomplished, he turned the occasion to the routine of "people don't like me, don't want me to be reelected, want to hurt me in the polls," etc. The fact that millions of Americans were at risk of dying was ignored and then he goes to the one and only thing he could possibly point to as having a degree of success since his election, the economy. Then just to follow his own repetitive script he again absurdly played the fake news card that in his mind was all he could come up with and was far more important than answering the question. The economy will survive over time, perhaps not on his timetable and admittedly not ideal, but in spite of his pathetic use of the phrase resurrecting the economic recovery to tie to his Easter postulate, people had and would continue to die. And more than ever during a public health crisis, citizens are highly dependent on the media for truthful information, from the president. Instead, invariably his comments turn very quickly to rally-speak as if he is the Big Brother leader in the George Orwell novel *1984* [91]exerting total dominance over citizens. The cancerous Trump tumor runs wild and even simple communication is missing, but noise and clutter is in abundance as he strives for martyrdom.

The Trump cancer attacks truth, but this Trump-created disease has also assaulted and paralyzed any ability for him to have an informed perspective and set priorities that benefit the country, not him. As the pandemic continued to grow in the US and around the world, Task Force scientists were placed in a position of continually correcting his statements that were exaggerated and of course provide Trump the opportunity to stroke himself. Trump takes great pride in calling the Covid-19 the hidden enemy when in reality it is staring all Americans directly in their faces. What is hidden is the truth. Like cancer, truth is camouflaged by any number of statements and actions by the Trump administration. Twisting words, ignoring facts and experts and deflecting questions is the routine when these questions could and should be answered with direct information. It is notable that Trump himself only has a minimal ability to think on his feet when pressed for answers. He rapidly falls back into his comfort zone of three or four talking points that have become so repetitive and lack substance that for many Americans his statements have no meaning at all.

One of these talking points is criticizing the Obama administration for most everything, and the Bush administration as well, and accusing these prior administrations of leaving him with messes that he had to inherit. A victim, remember? Many of his claims have been disproven, of course, and when they are or when material is discovered that demonstrate the Trump administration's mishandling of critical issues, they are deflected, dismissed or ignored. But without fail in the face of all information is to continue to use the false rhetoric. The Trump administration was briefed in 2017 concerning a playbook report[92] that outlined considerations for an early response to significant infectious diseases and other biological incidents , not unlike the Covid-19 pandemic currently infecting people around the globe.

The Trump administration has been critical of that report and have made statements regarding its lack of applicability because of more recent experience, *e.g.*, the Ebola epidemic. Trump taking the position that the Covid-19 pandemic could not have been expected dramatically misses the point, and the opportunity. Every new virus requires evaluation, study and approaches developed toward management. Therapeutics, and potential vaccines also require research and development, with accompanying studies to determine the medications' efficacy and safety. But the significant opportunity that was missed was not acting and not waiting to address supply chain organization, communication plans, stockpiling of critical personal protective material for healthcare providers and including guidelines for the release of these materials form the Strategic National Stockpile. In other words, making preparations in advance in such a fashion that would provide direction for decisions in anticipation of facing a pandemic, and not waiting and do everything at once, or not at all.

Instead, this administration continued to point blame elsewhere for its inadequacies, punctuated by Trump statements such as "I take no responsibility at all" when questioned about the lack of access for Covid-19 testing.[93] Once again he blamed the situation on the past when if he had taken action early and proactively in his tenure as president, based on the immediate warnings he was provided before and after he assumed office, the situation could have been addressed rather than rolling the dice and assume all is well. It was obviously more important to him at the time to continue to whine about the election, crowd size at his inauguration, deliver a message about "American carnage" and how unfair the media covered him. This behavior of avoidance of truth was necessarily the beginning of a trend as the Trump history illustrates that above all he believes he is the most important component for any topic, and situation and misses the realization that his version of American carnage he is creating is significant.

It should be with great gratitude that the country would benefit from the White House Covid-19 Task Force, chaired by Pence, to oversee management of the Covid-19 pandemic. With members from the CDC, FDA, NIH, Public Health Service, HHS, etc., and representative scientists such as Dr. Fauci[94], and Dr. Deborah Birx[95] bringing much needed reality and guidance for all. But as time passed, thanks to Trump and Pence in particular, messaging became confused, and non-Task Force members such as the White House press secretary,[96] the president's chief counselor[97] and assorted Republican Senators provided little intelligence for clarity and frequently added to the "communication carnage." Apparently there is an identity crisis as well for the members of the Task Force. When Apple's virtual assistant, Siri®, is asked to name the White House Coronavirus Task Force members, at least one choice response is, "I don't know who the band members are."

A significant Trump cancerous approach thus far in his years in office is to not pay attention to or even use the expertise of the intelligence community and other topic-specific experienced individuals. Rather, he is more inclined to be oriented to personal wins, and stable genius knowledge, toward building a border wall, romancing dictators, alienating long-standing global relationships, prohibiting certain minority groups from entering the country, defying the House and blocking documents to help in determining whether he had created acts that supported his pending impeachment. In the latter case, cooperation may have prevented the asterisk by his name in history that will now never be removed, but the public is still waiting for documents and information but will never know. Truth, a wonderful thing when it leads as opposed to it being manipulated or buried. As Irish playwright Oscar Wilde stated, "Man is least himself when he talks in his own person. Give him a mask, and he will tell you the truth." Perhaps Trump is aware of Wilde's warning of sorts and this may be why he chooses to ignore his administration's and CDC recommendations about wearing a mask in the time of the Covid-19 pandemic for fear of what he might say. On the other hand, he employs no filters now and his personality mask is all enveloping. The Trump cancer may have decided that its best defense in all matters is just lying to itself. Trump only believes what he says to himself and as he listens to his own lies his ability to recognize what is true is grossly impaired and maybe even lost forever.

Under Trump hope has also become a missing commodity. When truth is not a priority it is difficult for Americans to feel hopeful about the health of the country and how their own well-being is being relegated to an afterthought. This feeling is also shared by elected officials, even some from Trump's own political party who are so disenchanted with what is occurring that they are compelled to speak up. They are fearful of being viewed as complicit in contributing to the Trump cancer. They too must have hope that the increasing partisan divide encouraged by Trump and their own colleagues, will soon come to an end.

It is incredibly hard for people to come together to provide support when division seems to be the overriding theme and the repetitive chapter in the president's playbook. But those in the House and Senate as well as state and local leaders must be encouraged to keep the interests of their constituents at the forefront of decisions to manage the needs of the country, not only being reelected. That is a tough sell for many, but to not take that position predicts ongoing mismanagement, dysfunction and division. If all, or least enough of them, would just perform responsibly and institute a paradigm shift from the lack of governing in the Trump White House many questions will fall by the wayside at the time of their next election. When the president habitually glosses over facts or misrepresents them in favor of portraying himself in the best possible light, the needs of the country disappear quickly. As the centerpiece of false information, the Trump cancer does not embolden hope. It is up to concerned Americans to promote hope by becoming involved in their destiny in productive ways instead of becoming victims of division. It is important to engage with the representatives and senators who they have helped to elect as well as with those who have significant influence on civility and truth to move the country forward. Hope is needed. Hope is deserved. But only truth and productive action will serve as the catalysts for generating hope.

Although the Trump cancer thrives on lies and other false claims, there has been one statement he has made that all can possibly agree is true. It is one that an elementary school teacher would have no trouble using to demonstrate how to diagram a sentence to his/her students as opposed to the routine rambling orations from Trump that leaves one stupefied. His statement had a simple subject, verb and object. In a very strong manner when asked about the Covid-19 testing stumbling Trump responded, "I don't take responsibility at all."[98] He actually made a true statement. He takes responsibility for nothing other than what he perceives to be the outcome of his stable genius actions, facts be damned, and only those that fulfill his need for self-aggrandizement. But Dr. King's words come back to mind very quickly. "Likewise, if a man does not make truth a tantamount characteristic of his being, he dies as well."

*"The best way to not feel hopeless is to get up and do something.
Don't wait for good things to happen to you.
If you go out and make some good things happen,
you will fill the world with hope, you will fill yourself with hope."*

—————————— PRESIDENT BARACK OBAMA ——————————

Americans need to get up and do the right thing. Do what they know is required to get the country back on track. Go all in and do everything they can as individuals to restore hope for the future.

CHAPTER FOUR

This Cancer Is a Tactic, Not Just a Disease

"All warfare is based on deception. Hence, when we are able to attack, we must seem unable; when using our forces, we must appear inactive; when we are near, we must make the enemy believe we are far away; when far away, we must make him believe we are near."

SUN TZU, THE ART OF WAR

The *Art of War* is a book written by a Chinese military strategist, Sun Tzu, the origins of which date as far back as the 6th century BC. Over time his writings have become a document frequently consulted, often quoted, discussed and in some fashion has most likely even influenced military decisions and strategy by eastern and western leaders. To equate strategy as an overlay for what has taken place during the Trump tenure as president is far too kind, well actually, not even appropriate. Deception, on the other hand, is a finely-honed skill of the Trump cancer.

Strategy defined: the science and art of employing the political, economic, psychological, and military forces of a nation or group of nations to afford the maximum support to adopted policies in peace or war.[99] There is nothing about this definition that applies to Trump, his cognitive powers, his mindset or his actions. This definition makes clear that to effectively apply a strategy requires the employment of multiple areas of expertise as complementary support while executing well thought out and meaningful policies designed to achieve a common goal. The Trump cancer starts at the end of the definition by sighting his personal laser focus on the goal but not how to get there. Look at what he tweets and then think the opposite. To his own dismay he reveals much about himself to those who take the time to dissect his words and arrive at intent. But just as often intent is even lost and what is left are bizarre conspiracy theories and statements that cannot possibly be real, can they? Trump doesn't really seem to care if anyone supports his policies or not. He has surprised those around him many times by agreeing to one thing and then doing another. His goal is whatever benefits Trump. Just like cancer in the body, the Trump cancer does not discriminate. It doesn't matter what is damaged, who is hurt or what institutions, traditions and morals are trampled along the way.

The modus operandi intensely pursued by Trump is to surround himself with people who won't criticize him and do not offer alternatives that are critical of a Trump objective or idea. With that approach the Trump cancer can't be compromised. In the Trump administration these individuals represent a diverse cross-section of experienced and inexperienced people. The Trump cancer is reinforced as these supporters mistakenly do not require him to read and study material or even direct that he pay attention to their input in order to arrive at an informed opinion. In general, these folks applaud him at every opportunity. In the book written by former National Security Advisor John Bolton[100] there are many recollections presented about how he and others viewed the president's strategic missteps, his intellect and his unrestrained behaviors. The problem is, however, the public only sees the Trump cancer's tweets, voiced threats picked up by the media and some insight gained from the occasional leak from the White House. Vice president Pence is probably the most obvious example, voicing his unrestricted support as his constant over the top compliments and stroking of the Trump ego approaches a catalyst precipitating nausea for many. Pence's motivation is somewhat obvious as he wished to stay on the Trump Republican ticket for the 2020 election. Should this reelection bid fail, the Pence legacy as a Trump submissive lapdog does not bode well for any political future down the road. Why would it? The negativity that surrounds Pence will be far too great a mountain to climb as he is patently unbelievable. He represents to the public just another individual who puts personal objectives and lies above truth and responsibility.

As cancer in the body will resist attempts to deflect targeted regimens at the cellular level, the Trump cancer just as assuredly deflects responsibility for any of his actions or inactions. If Trump perceives he has a "win," well that's another matter even if truth prevails and it's not a win at all. In this sense the Trump cancer might also be termed the Trump distraction and its endless tactical execution is to use the deflections exercised to separate itself from everything not complimentary to his boasts. The Covid-19 pandemic provides clarity and an example of incompetence and lack of true leadership as Trump flaunted his scientific expertise and dismissal of all manner of evidence in terms of what was ahead for the country that authentically countered his proclamations. A careful analysis of his comments beginning in January 2020 and over subsequent months shows just how far the Trump cancer will go to bring all attention to the I/me view of the world. He played as an autocrat with boundaries defined by his attempts to show he was in charge, not Covid-19, and on every possible occasion he rolled out the personal credit for how well the country was doing in face of this humanitarian and economic crisis, *e.g.*, it will just disappear with warm weather. However, all truth illustrates his unbounded lack of presidential leadership, and certainly that is his to own. The Trump Twitter library shows just how uncertain, convoluted and inaccurate his opinions were, with grammar, punctuation and capitalizations as tweeted. Author comments are in italics:

January 24 - "Today I met with global health experts about the outbreak of a novel Covid-19 in China. We learned that the risk of transmission within the US is low at present. I will continue to work closely with US officials to ensure Americans are protected."

A good place to start an assessment. From the beginning he ignored the counsel of science.

January 30 - "Working closely with China and others on Covid-19 outbreak. Only 5 people in US, all in good recovery."

Keep in mind that Trump was still wrangling his trade deal with China so the motivation to compliment rather than criticize President Xi and China was in play. Also worth noting that he has admitted he knew more about the seriousness of the situation than he was admitting to the public.

During this period the impeachment trial was also taking place in the Republican controlled Senate and no doubt Trump may have viewed the threat of the Covid-19 as a distraction. The Senate voted to clear Trump of the Articles of Impeachment on February 5.

February 25 - "CDC and my Administration are doing a GREAT job of handling Covid-19, including the very closing of our borders to certain areas of the world. It was opposed by the Dems, "too soon," but turned out to be the correct decision. No matter how well we do, however the...Democrats talking point is that we are doing badly. If the virus disappeared tomorrow, they would say we did a really poor, and even incompetent, job. Not fair, but it is what it is. So far, by the way, we have not had one death. Let's keep it that way!"

Taking his recurrent attack on the Democrats with exaggerated and unsupported allegations in view of a healthcare crisis shows the Trump cancer focus was on the forthcoming election, not the health of the country's citizens.

The impact of the travel "ban" from China may have had a degree of positive impact in slowing Covid-19 from spreading around the US, but Trump's growing claims in early March began with "saved a lot of lives," to "probably tens of thousands," and by April had leaped to "hundreds of thousands."[101] The spread of the virus outside of China may have been slowed but it was by no means contained. The travel restriction imposed by Trump was not a ban at all as there were exceptions to his edict of travelers entering the US. And lest it be overlooked, this tweet was the first appearance of the now infamous quote, "it is what it is" when referencing the pandemic.

February 28 - "The Do Nothing Democrats were busy wasting time on the Immigration Hoax, & anything else they could do to make the Republican Party look bad, while I was busy calling early BORDER & FLIGHT closings, putting us way ahead in our battle with Covid-19. Dems called it VERY wrong!"

Once again, the Trump cancer politicized a growing problem for the country rather than focusing on a preparedness and management plan, as experts were identifying what was likely to occur in the US.

March 11 – "The Media should view this as a time of unity and strength. We have a common enemy, actually, an enemy of the World, the Covid-19. We must beat it as quickly and safely as possible. There is nothing more important to me than the life & safety of the United States!"

Really? His personal history and actions as president do not support his tweet. He made it abundantly clear on a variety of topics and levels that there is nothing more important to Trump than Trump, and his personal wealth of course. The one thing on the accomplishment ledger that he had to focus on for his reelection was the economy, regardless of how much direct impact he had on its growth, and it was "Safety" was a word he thought, maybe, a president should say.

Subsequent tweets, comments at briefings and answers to reporters' questions there and elsewhere, routinely raised topics that had nothing to do with the pandemic. Instead Trump retreated to his golden oldies criticizing Democrats, some by name like President Obama, Hillary Clinton, President Bush and of course misquoting people and data. Blame was in abundance directed toward anyone and anything that could be teed up by Trump, while responsibility or accountability accepted by the Trump administration was consistently missing.

Over the weeks and months, the Twitter trail was populated with false claims, accusations directed toward state governors, the media and Democrats of course, and Trump's participation at Task Force briefings became increasingly bizarre. In this instance the cancer was reaching across many boundaries of expertise within the government that required others to repeatedly provide clarity in what most often became a politically correct deferral to the Trump position in spite of the information he was delivering. Trump wanted desperately to portray how well he was guiding the federal government's management of the exploding crisis, but much the opposite was displayed. He was critical of actions at the state level even though governors were demonstrating far more leadership than Trump. The supply chain conflicts, pitting the states against the Federal Emergency Management Agency (FEMA) and other agencies, provided fodder for the Trump cancer to abdicate responsibility regarding life-saving supplies by stating, "we are not a shipping clerk."[102]

Along the way Trump flipped his adoration of President Xi and China began to criticize both, implying that officials there were not being honest about what had occurred about the discovery of the coronavirus (later confirmed), and he floated his own brand of a conspiracy theory about the dishonesty about the release of the virus. This theory ignored the World Health Organization (WHO) warning that had come months before. Trump implied that the "China virus" constituted the development of a man-made weapon to be inflicted on the US, and like a good soldier this was reinforced by Secretary of State Mike Pompeo. "The best experts so far seem to think it was man-made. I have no reason to disbelieve that at this point." When reminded that his opinion did not line up with intelligence agencies Pompeo said, "I've seen what the intelligence community has said. I have no reason to believe that they've got it wrong."[103] Classic, just classic, but probably not a technique learned during his time at West Point and Harvard.

Thus, the misbehavior of China in terms of transparency escalated in the mind of the stable genius that it was something else. He criticized the WHO for "favoring" China and threatened to withdraw US funding of this historic and effective organization. He criticized members of Congress. He continued his sweep of removing agency and department Inspector Generals. He made questionable appointments that even on the surface appeared to be politically motivated rather than appropriate vetting of individuals for the experience, skills and qualifications for the positions in question. This was by no means new behavior as he simply continued a disregard for building a functioning government in favor of crafting political alliances and suggesting promises he couldn't really deliver. Job security was never assumed in the Trump sphere. If there was an opportunity to deflect any criticism of him toward others, he grabbed it with gusto. It's the historic Trump way and in this classically mishandled situation of Covid-19 the opportunity for questioning and criticism of his mismanagement was significant. The Trump cancer was out of control and effectively creating its own pandemic spread of ill-conceived political moves.

The Trump deflection tactic was in full view and the coming deflection pivot on the horizon became increasingly predictable. The economy was soon to get totally out of his influence as the Covid-19 situation grew, with "sheltering in place" directions from individual states and the mitigation guidance was provided by the CDC. Businesses shut down, small and large, diagnosed cases grew exponentially and the number of deaths increased across the country, with certain notable "hotspots" in several states. Unemployment figures steadily increased week after week across all demographics. In spite of the financial stimulus packages made available, the process of access proved difficult and the communications from the federal government to navigate the process were lacking in clear detail as loan applications grew as did the general frustration for businesses in some sectors. Trump talked more about the economy than any expression of true empathy for the people who were sick and dying from Covid-19 or for the medical professionals and first responders on the front lines caring for victims and trying hard to make a difference as they continued to face a shortage of equipment and supplies. It was if he really just didn't care about stepping up and leading to resolve desperate situations or problems. Oh, how soon we forget…"I take no responsibility at all."

Task Force briefings continued to throw out numbers of what equipment and supplies were being made available, but states and hospitals found it hard to identify where the supplies were to be found. The number of tests available was also a common subject but like the direct PPE supplies and ventilators they were difficult to find and in spite of the pleas for contact tracing from the scientists the topic was consistently not addressed with a plan and on some occasions never mentioned at all in the briefings, except by the media. Derogatory remarks and contradictions continued to flow from Trump as well as his braggadocio about his corporate friends jumping into the fray by manufacturing items needed to combat the shortages surrounding the slopping administration response to the virus in the first place. The common thread appears once again. Tactically the "I" reference was rolled out as the centerpiece for Trump to take credit for everything, except mistakes and lack of action, of course. What he didn't acknowledge was how, without any involvement from him, the country, businesses and citizens, were coming together to produce materials, employ mitigation techniques and in general show an appreciation for what could be accomplished together and by following the direction of science. Of note is that this type of coming together was not exclusive to the US, as evidence mounted how similar activities were taking place in other countries as humanity was far more important than politics.

To further provide spotlight moments for Trump he employed the tactic of using his vast scientific knowledge to advocate bizarre therapeutic interventions to fight Covid-19. First it was a focused and repetitive bannering of the use of a highly effective anti-malaria drug, hydroxychloroquine that anecdotally was believed to be a possible solution. Specific safety and efficacy studies for this use did not exist at the time, and the suggested combination with the anti-infective azithromycin[104] was not clinically proven. Scientists and clinicians, however, continued to try and temper his remarks, particularly around potential safety concerns and in particular negative cardiovascular events. But Trump, ever eager to draw focus towards himself, announced that he had, was (he changed the verb frequently), personally ingested the questionable drug for two weeks with no negative effects and he "felt great." Trump even blurted out more of his expertise by referring to azithromycin as Z-Pak, "we call it Z-Pak." But once again he was off base. The Z-Pak introduced years ago, was a dosing friendly blister package that made it simple for patients to keep track of taking a recommended dosage over a period of days as it was prescribed by physicians for several bacterial indications including strep throat. Many hospitalized Covid-19 patients were given hydroxychloroquine because of Trump's continual hype for its use, voiced as "what have you got to lose," with the implication that an individual is going to die anyway so why not. It was a pathetic attempt to appear as a hero, be out front and a questionable bid to exert control. Evaluation of patients who were given the combination of hydroxychloroquine and azithromycin did not reveal any significant therapeutic effect, but alarmingly did show a significant incidence of dangerous cardiac events. What great leadership in action by Trump that accomplished nothing but put him in a spotlight, and this is only one such example. Later, however, to just put a punctuation point on the Trump medical expertise, a study was published in the internationally renowned medical journal *The Lancet*. In this observational study of over 96,000 patients each of the drug regimens of chloroquine or hydroxychloroquine alone or in combination with a macrolide was associated with an increased hazard for clinically significant occurrence of ventricular arrhythmias and increased risk of in-hospital death with Covid-19.[105] Although this study was later refuted, ongoing evidence supported the original position taken in this article.

America's concern was growing, jobs were being lost at an alarming rate or people found their means of employment income being furloughed for an indeterminable period of time. The personal and economic toll of the virus continued to increase and the ability of families to be together and put food on their table at home became a growing concern for many. Private concerns stepped up to provide food pickups and once again received little acknowledgement in a public way from the administration. Further, when three significant scientists and medical professionals (Dr. Robert Redfield, CDC director, Dr. Stephen Hahn, FDA commissioner, and Dr. Anthony Fauci, Director of NIAID), all members of the White House Covid-19 Task Force, made the decision to self-quarantine because they had had contact with White House staff who had received a positive Covid-19 test, their responsible action was not mentioned by Trump, but he reassured the world that he felt great and that he had been tested and doesn't need to wear a mask. Even in the face of clear evidence of the fact that the virus had invaded "his home" and wasn't magically disappearing, he continued to contradict what highly knowledgeable scientists were projecting in terms of the likelihood of increased cases, and deaths. Instead, it was about encouraging a "reopening" of the country to rescue the economy, and potentially, of course, rescue his reelection.

The Trump cancer was outwardly using the economy as the deflection to showcase his concern for getting people back to work, not their health but "his" economy. But the reality was he was politicizing a critical health situation, the pandemic, as a means of once again speaking to his base and his cronies in an attempt to stop the hemorrhaging of a disorganized reelection bid. In spite of the billions of dollars approved by Congress to help individuals and businesses, including big business bail outs Trump, in whatever forum he chose, was willing to let others deal with Covid-19 and his failures, and he abdicated any personal responsibility in dealing with the situation. As he has shown he is so prone to do in troublesome situations the Trump cancer created another smokescreen deflection to draw attention elsewhere, particularly as he felt it would benefit him personally. In the case of Covid-19, the economy was the deflection and evidence-based assessments of more people dying and would die became a "cost of doing business." He willingly accepted this downside of rushing to reopen the country and shifting focus to the single thing he would represent as an accomplishment of his presidency.

Democracy's a very fragile thing. You have to take care of democracy. As soon as you stop being responsible to it and allow it to turn into scare tactics, it's no longer democracy, is it? It's something else. It may be an inch away from totalitarianism.

——————————— SAM SHEPARD ———————————

Trump's autocratic approach to "governing" was his deep-seated personal belief that his opinion was more important than any other, and that he would succeed no matter what others may say or feel. He has the expectation that everyone should bow to his authority, Republicans, Democrats it doesn't matter. He is right after all. He believes he has the power to criticize the history of the country, the dedicated founders, those who produced classic legislation that would influence the country's place in the world as well as how Americans would thank him for his accomplishments in office. Totalitarianism? Trump is not just inching towards it, he expects it. He's expecting his statues, adoration from all around the world, and expressions of unequivocal gratitude for allowing Americans his genius as president of the country while he destroyed democracy in the US.

Americans were worried about how the pandemic was impacting their lives both near- and long-term, but the person most in fear was Trump himself and it was not about succumbing to the coronavirus himself. There was little positive coming out of his administration because of the virus' detrimental impact on society and business as one distinct possibility, and Trump himself was indeed in a state of fear if not panic for his future. The walls were closing in, his public behavior showed less and less patience with legitimate challenges to his policy positions by members of Congress, the media and citizens who were fearful for their lives and the lives of their family members. He demonstrated his preoccupation with himself when at a Task Force briefing NBC reporter Peter Alexander asked a serious but "high lobbed softball" question that a leader would have pounced on with a meaningful response and knocked out of the park. The question was what he could say to Americans who were watching him in that moment and who are scared? Instead of showing leadership he responded angrily.

> *"I say that you are a terrible reporter, that's what I say. I think it's a very nasty question. I think it's a very bad signal that you are putting out to the American people. They're looking for answers and they're looking for hope. And you're doing sensationalism and the same with NBC and Concast (sic)—I don't call it Comcast I call it Concast. Let me just, who do you work, let me just say something. That's really bad reporting. And you ought to get back to reporting instead of sensationalism. Let's see if it works. It might and it might not. I happen to feel good about it, but who knows? I've been right a lot."*[106]

This is not the first or only example of Trump missing the big picture. He didn't answer the question, but instead he went to his favored short list of responses, and in this case attacking the reporter and his employer. To what purpose? Alexander had prefaced his question with the facts that were known at that moment in terms of the number of cases and deaths. Covid-19 was a top of mind fear for all and here was an opportunity for Trump to appear empathetic and presidential. But once again he failed on both counts. People were desperate for credible information so rather than recognize this particular occasion as an opportunity Trump fell back into his typical tough guy mode and shanked a foul ball. To his credit the reporter did not take the Trump cancer's bait and followed up in an endeavor to provide Trump with another chance to give a meaningful response to the question. Trump's response was an angry stare, a smirk and a quick turn to a different reporter in the room. The question remained unanswered. The country did need information, but the president didn't really seem to care.

Even when the CDC provided a comprehensive package of guidelines to the administration regarding the reopening of the country the White House reaction was one of rejection. This was apparently because it was viewed as too conservative, advocated actions that did not fit the Trump reopening scheme that was more about dollars and cents instead of saving lives, and not as aggressive as Trump desired for a "rapid" recovery. The White House guidelines were crafted with the economy, and the forthcoming election, as the underlying foundation. The tactic of autocratic authority was designed to bend all those in his purview to bow to his absolute knowledge, while at the same time he continued to make bizarre statements, recant them and then revisit them later when the spirit moved him. But the underlying effect fit his deflection tactic from Covid-19 and instead he was all about the election and putting his face front and center with his base. He had proven in the past that he could lie and be elected and in the face of the virus and its impact on the members of his base, he brought out the favored talking point of his incredible abilities, and no matter what the Democrats attempt, he termed Covid-19 a hoax and he will "keep" America great. Even son Eric joined the misinformation party and accused Democrats of "milking" coronavirus lockdowns to win the election.[107] Trump has trained his offspring well, as Don Jr., Eric and Ivanka are equally adept at furthering their father's agenda and frequently even going off script, another Trump trait, with misstatements of their own. Even son-in-law Jared Kushner gets in the game.

Speaking of Jared, at one point he was asked in an interview with *Time* magazine whether he could acknowledge that the 2020 presidential election would take place as scheduled on November 3. Raising more than a few eyebrows he responded that "I'm not sure I can commit one way or the other, but right now that's the plan."[108] It was the words "right now" that became a point of focus, with concern that the Trump administration may actually attempt to delay the election or at least may be considering it. Kushner later stated that he was not involved in any discussions about changing the date of the election. So not that this walk back provided any real clarification in fact, but it did demonstrate that Jared, like his father-in-law, was light on an understanding of the Constitution. The president does not have the authority to delay or cancel an election.

As the deflection distractions and delusional tweets and statements are directed toward experts, both governmental and scientific, his enemies and the public, what is clear is that any attempt to predict where Trump will turn next is quite impossible. It is similar to an ant crawling around your picnic lunch and trying to predict what direction its somewhat spasmic perambulations will terminate next, cole slaw, potato chips or hot dogs. There is no way to know nor do the ants care, and neither does Trump. Nevertheless, the one constant is his playing to the camera, the headlines and making his "ant-like" moves to deliver his authoritarian if not dictatorial comments. "Don't confuse me with the facts," is an uncontrollable and driving force of his personality that Trump constantly provides controversy. He thrives on controversy as he must believe it places him on solid ground with this 2016 voting base. Remember that that campaign, and since, thrives on things he makes up or on some perverted level he believes are true. The Trump cancer believes that the more the same thing is said the voting public will cluster to his wisdom. The problem with that is that his statements are so routinely bizarre and unsubstantiated that those who believe his every word may aspire to his brand of wisdom and still execute their vote Trump. Consider the intellectual gymnastics below:

"If ISIL ever attack the Vatican the Pope will be hoping and praying, I'm the President."[109] "Disloyal Republicans are far more difficult than Crooked Hillary. They came at you from all sides. They don't know how to win. I will teach them."[110] "Nobody knew that health care could be so complicated."[111]

Perhaps the Trump cancer should not rely so heavily on the "wisdom of his crowd" and respect the following conclusion from author James Sirowiecki. "The decisions that democracies make may not demonstrate the wisdom of the crowd. The decision to make them democratically does."[112] In other words Trump should put his id aside. No one should care about the world according to Trump. Respect the Constitution. Respect the power and right of individual thought. Respect the process of voting choice. Respect the outcome of the total of all who vote and respect their decisions. He needs to understand what democracy means and the inherent positive benefits of motivation rather than instigation

What escapes Trump, however, is that there are millions of Americans who shake their heads in disbelief and have their negative viewpoints towards him reinforced in terms of how many feel he is unfit to be president. They look forward to doing their part as individuals to defeat him and his band of Senate and administration lackies in November 2020 and yes, truly making America great again because it is about the people. Although Trump can wear his oversized MAGA hat as his self-awarded badge of honor, he has dragged the country down at most every opportunity and demonstrated to the world that he is far from competent to be "the leader of the free world." The distractions he creates are wide ranging. For example, he can go off the rails at any time. "Dishwashers. You didn't have any water, the people that do the dishes. You press it and it goes again, and you do it again and again. So, you might as well give them the water because you'll end up using less water. So, we made it so dishwashers now have a lot more water. And in many places, in most places of the country, water is not a problem. They don't know what to do with it. It's called rain. They don't have a problem."[113] In the middle of a pandemic with no national plan, this is what concerns the president.

The tactical distractions and deformed thoughts of this cancer just don't cease, and each day Americans and the world are offered something more outrageous. As the Trump cancer paranoia ramps up its illogical and most frequently nonsensical lack of civility, he applies no limits or filters to what action he may invoke or statement that may appear. But be assured that at the root of his rants, undocumented opinions, ignorance of governing and lack of control there is a common ground to his chaos. The deflections and bewilderments of this cancer are based on personal and political motivations not the interests of the country. Anything and anyone are targets for Trump's baseless attacks as the thought of defeat in the next election is just too large a blow to his narcissistic personality. Trump has no vision, only impulsive reactions. He was surprised that he was elected in the first place, a mistake of incredible proportions. He knew that of course but grabbing power at this level was too much of an attraction.

In the history of his first term Trump himself consistently illustrates just how unqualified he was to even be considered as the best the Republican Party could propose for America. His offensive style, language and lies in no way reflect favorably on anyone in a leadership position, past or present, and that is the problem, or at least one prevailing problem of significance. Trump has proven that leadership is not in his DNA. He has placed himself on a pedestal that offers no possibility or guarantee for him to be perceived as a leader or even a truthful messenger. He thinks the opposite of course but sitting behind an historic desk is just not enough. It is impossible to predict what the topics of the day will be as often they occur to him in the middle of the night as he watches television and lines up his tweets for the day or on the spot as he reacts to news reports. If he didn't watch television so many hours of each day would he be a more responsible president? It is hard to imagine that that would even be a possibility. There is no order or logic to how he exposes himself and his intellect each day. Rarely are true facts communicated as opposed to childish criticisms of others, accusations of all types made against those who oppose him or are not loyal to him, or in some way do not bow to his absurd thoughts and proclamations. But a careful look also reveals that he incredibly quickly takes out his ire on anyone who criticizes him or disagrees with him, much as a child throwing a tantrum.

The looming 2020 election opened the floodgates for deflections as even more scrutiny was being applied to what the Trump cancer had done and was doing and that scrutiny, in spite of his accusations, was coming from many quarters. The country has seen and heard that nothing is off limits. No one is off limits. Facts and truth are unimportant. He put the ongoing health pandemic aside because, of course, he had convinced himself he handled it magnificently initially with his China travel ban and repeatedly says so, because after all, "I've been right a lot." This sort of narcissistic approach can also be linked to his repetitive messaging, or propaganda in action. Trump is a master of exploiting propaganda in the best traditions of Hitler and Nazi Germany when the message from Hitler was the promotion and recruitment of the superior and unpolluted Aryan master race.

Propaganda in its purest form presents information that is biased and misleading and used to publicize a particular political cause or point of view that negates all others. Truth is not a required component of the message because the proponents of propaganda don't recognize alternative thought because the manipulation of people and opinion is the desired end point. The Trump base of supporters uses cable and social media as a means of self-selecting the information that meets their psychological and sociological needs. In mass communications this is known as the uses and gratification theory and is associated with formation of attitudes based on individuals' expectations of media content. Trump uses propaganda as a form of persuasion to influence attitudes and beliefs to demean if not injure people and institutions, and of course, to demonstrate his "intelligence." But persuasion can also be used in an intentional way to mislead. In the Orwell novel *1984* 8[8] the author professed that in a totalitarian state a propaganda campaign has the intent to have unchallenged control over information to the point that whatever is being pushed out to the masses defines reality, *i.e.*, accepting false information as true. Sound familiar? The I-Party of Trump is following that very process. There are many who steadfastly believe that whatever he says is indeed true. Orwell also uses the term "doublethink" that describes "the power of holding two contradictory beliefs in one's mind simultaneously and accepting both of them." This too is representative of Trump as in his world he routinely presents multiple hypocritical misspeak, usually in the same fragmented sentence.

The Trump cancer tries to persuade people all the time in one way or another. Persuasion is an outcome, after all, of saying things or making promises that meet the needs of the audience. In this case Trump thinks his needs are most important and his form of persuasion is bringing supporters to his needs without really caring about the audience needs. His approach is just the opposite what true persuasion should strive for but "what 's in it for me" is the Trump world. The only dependence he seeks is a vote. It is not a two-way form of communication between himself and anyone else… ever. Many supporters don't see the manipulative form of persuasion being directed toward them, and others don't apparently care. The

Trump cancer invades every host it can find and speaking truth is not what he believes to be most important. He is only looking for the reaction/action that will be most beneficial to him by telling potential supporters what they need, telling them he will provide those things and then ultimately delivering nothing beyond what he wants and expecting them to push the message out to others. "I know more than the generals, the scientists, the Democrats" and believing he knows more than even more experienced members of his own Party. This is the prevailing foundation of his persuasion messages. Think about his statements about race, police brutality, protests, the pandemic, his political opponents, laws, the courts; the cross he bears is knowing everything about everything.

Trump had long been suspected of having racist tendencies throughout his life and with the protests across the country in recent history racist orientation and statements have stood out in dramatic ways. At one point his attacks on President Obama seemed to have taken over his every thought and criticism. Obamagate? There was no basis for his accusations but when has that ever deterred him. False claims are the basis for his life, and in his position as president. As the dissatisfaction grew with his haphazard approach to the pandemic, Trump knew he was drowning and treading water was becoming more and more difficult. He retreated to defining any issue as the fault of others. He continued his patented behavior of firing people who he perceived as threats as they operated responsibly with foundational truth and ethics, attributes uncommon to him. His string of Friday night firings of several inspector generals who were functioning as required were just the latest in a much larger and troublesome problem. Of all the Senate Republicans, Mitt Romney was the most vocal in establishing his concern about what he termed Trump's removal of multiple inspectors general. "Doing so without good cause chills the independence essential to their purpose. It is a threat to accountable democracy and a fissure in the constitutional balance of power."[114] Trump's Twitter response to Romney complete with a video montage, "LOSER!"[115] The child at play; Trump, not Romney. As time passes it will become fascinating to watch Trump's reaction when references are made to the "loser president."

The Trump cancer has consistently, a word not easily to applied to this presidency, resisted all oversight by Congress of his personal behavior, the executive branch, and many federal agencies. Trump has run roughshod over the system of checks and balances and separation of powers of the three branches of government as outlined in the Constitution. He has even been aided, or at least supported, by Attorney General William Barr who has personally harnessed Trump's chameleon antics that are being questioned as well. Just as the most debilitating cancer invades the cells of its host, the Trump cancer has removed or shelved the overseers of the intelligence community, the Pentagon, and the Departments of Health, Transportation and State. Republicans in the Senate have been mute, unconcerned about what was occurring but once again demonstrating their fear of some type of reprisal against them by Trump should they speak out. Republicans in the Senate in particular have given up independent thought and have abandoned those who have elected them and for that matter the country as a whole and instead hide behind the "wall" built in the Senate by Mitch McConnell.

In concept, and with a demonstrable lack of practical knowledge and understanding, the Trump cancer has shown its lack of respect for the importance of executive branch oversight which, if he could take the time to understand, might at times even be a benefit to his presidency.

"If men were angels, no government would be necessary. If angels were to govern men, neither external nor internal controls on government would be necessary. In framing a government which is to be administered by men over men, the great difficulty lies in this: you must first enable the government to control the governed; and in the next place oblige it to control itself."[116]

It isn't that the Trump cancer just was not responding to the concept of oversight. The problem is deeper than that. He has endlessly portrayed that his deepest belief is that his knowledge is superior to all others. He believes that he could/should not be challenged. He believes that any action he chooses to take is to be accepted without question. He believes that the Constitution provides him with unlimited power. If oversight did not exist, even if a Congressional committee investigation resulted in a clean slate, the process of having a check on the executive branch is necessary and appropriate. Without oversight, the Trump cancer would move unrestrained into a full-blown authoritarian incursion on the country. By Trump blocking oversight the incursion is only delayed. He has made a mutation of the DOJ into a Barr-whatever-the-president-wants agency. He finds people who will oppose credible experts and the result is information chaos.

As stated in Federalist 51, James Madison suggests that there must be a balance throughout the entirety of the government. Without that balance "liberty will be in peril and chaos will take over." Trump's challenge to balance has pervaded his administration's actions, and certainly his attempts at governing. Thinking only about how he has resisted Congressional subpoenas, how he has manipulated the judicial branch and how he has attempted, in numerous ways, to use his office to ignore the Constitution and attempt to take positions of authority where he quite literally has none, chaos is a kind description of the situation Americans have and will continue to face. It is also quite apparent that he has put liberty in peril. He has used unwarranted and illegal powerplays as tactics that negatively pervade government agencies. His nepotism appointments have created ongoing chaos, most notably from son-in-law Jared who was given incredible yet inappropriate authority over multiple areas based on no experience and with subsequently no significant accomplishments to count. Like his father-in-law Kushner also touted the Covid-19 pandemic as a hoax and identified it as "more about public psychology than a health reality."[117] Amazing, and this perspective can't be blamed on the Trump genome.

During the 2016 campaign Trump seemed to enliven his base by stressing his great success in business that would serve him well as president. Whatever business acumen he assumed he had it became apparent that what he indeed potentially had brought with him was a disregard for the rule of law, a belief he could exert his supreme authority over everything and everybody, ala his appreciation of dictators around the world, and an unrestrained assault on the intelligence community and multiple federal agencies. He has manipulated the Department of Justice, disrespected the Bill of Rights and has defied Congress at every turn. In the throes of the pandemic crisis he showed his manipulative management skills as he played both sides of the medical treatment needs equation by threatening state governors, and in the next breath threw the ball to them when it was clear he really had no plan at all. Again, that repetitive style of blaming others and under no circumstances accept responsibility.

Of particular concern to all those who respect the Constitution and how the county is intended to be governed is his maneuvering, scheming and exploitation of others. Notable examples include the shielding of documents during the Mueller investigation that might be related to his ties to Russia and President Putin during the 2016 election, as well as numerous documents and witnesses requested by House judiciary committee during its impeachment inquiry proceedings. The Trump cancer was on the move on all fronts. He blocked key individuals from testifying before committees, slandered the reputations of those who had served the country long before his election and since and prevented many individuals in the administration from actually providing their truthful and potentially damaging testimony; distractions and deflections that served his agenda well by ignoring the rule of law. And how did he further use all of these visible deflections? He implied that his impeachment trial distracted him and thus influenced late or bad decisions as the pandemic was becoming more real each day. What distracted him was the damage to his ego. Nice try, but the fix was in. A Republican majority in the Senate acquitted him of the Articles of Impeachment submitted by the House at the time of the trial.

The Republican majority in the Senate, and others of the Republican cohort, along with the Trump legal team, were not concerned about the Trump cancer blockage of people and evidence. These co-obstructionists made the argument that all the subpoenas and document requests could/should be decided in the courts as united gaslighting for not adhering to the subpoenas or providing documents. Anyone with a speck of intelligence could see through this position as just a means of deflecting decisions until after the November election and perhaps even longer. This ongoing procedural sham unfolded during the trial on a daily basis in spite of the evidence presented. The Trump cancer had decidedly placed its thumb on the scales of justice, and the cancer's allies trampled over the other branches of government that were intended to be separate and not his personal toys to be used in a tactical and political way. The disease continued to spread unchecked.

The Trump cancer can never overdose on attention. Trump craves it. He creates situations that both knowingly and unknowingly generate media attention. He obsesses on Twitter posts whether there is any basis in fact, or truth about what he types into his phone. When challenged and asked to substantiate his statements he just moves on to a new lie or claim, *i.e.*, deflection, but he also reverts back to beating old and tired accusatory verbal drums he has used endlessly when threatened. The visibility of this tactic is in full effect and on each occasion, he is undoubtedly quite proud.

Case in point:

As pressure built up on the increasing potential that, according to multiple polls, Trump's 2020 reelection prospect was in trouble and over time the gloomy forecast was less and less promising. The Trump cancer focused his preoccupation on mail-in voting, and the potential for voter fraud, just as he had done after the 2016 election, the election he had called rigged" even before it had taken place. At the time he must have felt that his statements provided great cover for his fear or perhaps understanding that he would lose. After he was elected, he established a Presidential Advisory Commission on Election Integrity to investigate voter fraud as he professed that there had been 3-5 million illegal votes, particularly by immigrants, which he stated as the reason he lost the popular vote. The missing popularity blow to his ego was just too much to just move on.

The Commission was led by Republican leaders, Vice President Pence as chair, and Kansas Secretary of State, Kris Kobach. The Commission's "work" officially began on May 11, 2017 and was disbanded January 3, 2018. The methodology, although by reasonable authoritative research standards was not ideal, and was centered on requesting voter registration names from each state. On the surface this was an invasion of records that were kept for state purposes and the request was resisted by the majority of states. Ultimately no report was issued, and no evidence was presented to the Commission that would provide verification of Trump's voter fraud claims. Also, it is unclear whether records were ever presented to document double voting, another false claim. So once again a failed, if not embarrassing, Trump cancer tactic in terms of proving his bogus claim, but successful in creating a distraction at the time he was avoiding early and more serious concerns about his administration.

It's apparent that a lesson was not learned, facts accepted, or a teachable moment acknowledged and once again the Trump cancer took up the voter fraud torch in advance of the 2020 election. This time, however, it was a distraction to take away attention from the failed pandemic response and the economy. Trump continued to make unsubstantiated claims of past voter fraud and his prediction of widespread corruption to be realized in the results of the 2020 election. He did not lean too hard on his past corruption reference as it raises any number of Trump administration actions. A variation on his previous tactic to be sure, but a tactic designed to gin up his base. His claims were not new subjects for his tweets, but six months ahead of the election he was already building up his claims for an election loss for a second term. A tweet mid-summer at a point when his support appeared to be degrading, went even further:

"With Universal Main-In Voting (not Absentee Voting, which is good), 2020 will be the most INACCURAGE & FRADULENT Election. It will be a great embarrassment to the USA. Delay the Election until people can properly, securely and safely vote???"[118]

Was a suggestion of delaying the election just another shiny object tossed out to deflect attention from other matters on the day of the funeral for Congressmen John Lewis, attended by three former presidents but not Trump? Perhaps, but the president overlooks the fact that as specified in the Constitution that the Congress sets the date for the election and he alone can't change that direction. Isn't it interesting that he accuses mail-in voting as inherently a fraudulent process and yet absentee voting, by mail, is good? Someone needs to tell him absentee votes are mailed. Shortly after this early morning tweet it was noted a significant level of pushback occurred including from Republicans. But the Trump cancer was not through with the topic of voter fraud this day.

"I don't want to see the projected winner a week after November 3, or a month or frankly with litigation and everything else that can happen a year or years before you ever even know who won the election."[119]

The above statement was in answer to a media question about delaying the election, when Trump launched into what was clearly a prepared attack on mail-in voting. Of significance in his remarks is that he was promoting an election challenge by suggesting a delayed result, and he surfaced the term litigation which of course could inject a further level of delay. The US Election Assistance Commission's (EAC) 2016 Election Administration and Voting Survey Report[120] stated that 63 percent of the citizen voting age population voted in the presidential election or 140,114,502 voters. Of this number 41 percent cast their vote prior to Election Day either by absentee or in-person early voting. The pandemic has raised serious concerns on how voters can place in-person votes before or on Election Day and how many will choose that option in spite of potential risks to their health. Mail-in voting in one form or another has been facilitated in many states in the past and has not surfaced issues of any significance in terms of voter fraud. Prior to the pandemic Trump apparently would have still raised fraud as a reason for a defeat at the polls in November 2020. Again, it is important to remember that Trump's own Commission investigating the 2016 election showed no voter fraud or substantiated the additional Trump claim of double voting, but leading up to the 2020 election he has squarely set the stage for not accepting a November 3 defeat.

Because election administration is a responsibility placed with each state it remains to be seen the degree of commonality in procedures for voting in the 2020 election. Each state will respond with innovation to certify the vote and the procedures put in place to assure both voter protection and the vote. Of course, the added layer of oversight and procedures that will be required for the states to design and implement because of Covid-19 are significant. If the president were someone other than Trump would the country witness a more compassionate and understanding approach to voting procedures in the face of the pandemic? Like with most things, the Trump cancer does not exhibit or care about either of these attributes. The precedents for successful elections in a time of crisis, *e.g.*, the Civil War, the flu pandemic of 1918, World Wars I & II, are significant in number.

Nearly four years out from his inauguration Trump's continued use of the words voter fraud and his inference of a rigged election begs a question that the media rarely asks. "Mr. President, if the decision was made that mail-in votes was the methodology to be used for voting in the face of the Covid-19 crisis, and the result of the election was that you had won, would it still be a rigged election? If everything you have been accusing states of regarding mail-in voting over many months became "reality,", couldn't the opposition candidate make the same claims about the election outcome?" Undoubtedly the Tin Man before meeting Oz would present a better argument than the president could conjure up. Stay tuned. Don't be surprised if in a post-election loss scenario, he may also accuse those who "risked their lives" by voting in person in the face of the pandemic were part of a radical left-wing conspiracy and aren't real people, or some equally odd and demented claim.

Facing the reality that even in the pandemic environment situation when his presumed opponent cannot, chooses not, to hit the open road, Trump turns every "official" presidential trip into a campaign event. He faced the reality, or at minimum was fearful about it, that he was not viewed favorably outside of his base of support. The very thought that the popular vote would demonstrate to an even larger extent than in 2016 that his current opponent was "more popular" is just too much for him to accept. To add more misery as Trump lay awake at night with this phone on his pillow, in deciding two cases[121] the Supreme Court unanimously ruled that states may require presidential electors to support its winner of the popular vote. Thus, the popular vote can loom large over any success, or failure of Trump's reelection bid.

Mail-in voting in the face of the ongoing uncertainties of Covid-19 is not an invitation to voter fraud in spite of the discord that Trump clearly intends to escalate with his base. Any attempt to "ban" mail in voting was really more about an attempt to suppress voters who are more likely to vote against him and to continue his chaos approach to the world. The demographics of this group cross many segments of the voting public but even with that recognition Trump was just trying to tamp down all potential negative occurrences toward him. Boiled down to the essence of the Trump cancer's purpose, controlling the vote is a direct attack on the foundation of our democracy. Forget that the freedom to vote is provided through the Constitution (Amendments 15, 19 and 26), and in addition that states are given the latitude to establish qualifications for voting as well as the methodology that will be used. Consider rulings by the Supreme Court of the United States protecting citizen voting rights:

In *Reynolds v. Sims*[122] Chief Justice Earl Warren gave the opinion that "…the right to vote freely for the candidate of one's choice is of the essence of a democratic society, and any restrictions on that right strike at the heart of representative government."

In *Wesberry v. Sanders*[123] Justice Hugo Black opined, "No right is more precious in a free country than that of having a voice in the election of those who make the laws under which, as good citizens, we must live. Other rights, even the most basic, are illusory if the right to vote is undermined."

The Trump cancer parochial negative focus on mail-in voting is about his candidacy for a second term not a general concern about some change that should be universally applied from this point forward. What has received relatively little attention is that any degree of his suppression of voter activity would, by default, have an impact on all other races for state and local elections as well, including candidates of his own Party at the federal level. But of course, it's all about him, isn't it? It does make one wonder whether his advisers are presenting that potentially negative outcome to him and if so, is it like most other contrary opinions and is just being dismissed. Most likely, of course as the election is just about him. He is majestically obsessed with his own "success" and suppressing voters could most likely even threaten maintaining the Republican majority in the Senate. As much as he would like to control how every American should vote he overlooks the fact that voting is a right and highly valued by US citizens.

He has continued to attack his 2016 opponent, to what end, and is unable to withstand the fact that he was "not popular" by significantly losing the popular vote. More recently he was shown to be less liked than the leading pandemic scientist, Dr. Fauci, and there is considerable information that he doesn't focus on in terms of what might change opinions by the voting public prior to the 2020 election. The word pathetic comes to mind but its application to Trump could imply some level of compassion for his self-constructed situation.

The lack of leadership Trump exhibited during the early months of the pandemic, his outward disregard for his administration's and the CDC's guidelines to deal with the spread of Covid-19, and his arguments with governors who had been rebuked by him as they made decisions for their states etc., contributed to his fast becoming the poster boy for any manner or disorganized management and failed leadership. Making the voter fraud tactic front and center was all about delegitimizing an election that hadn't taken place. Even though mail-in voting had been used successfully by several states for some time, and the absentee voting procedures working well, Trump decided to question success in anticipation of his own failure.

There is something to be said for self-fulfilling prophecies.

As he did in 2016 Trump has erected his all-encompassing voting fraud smokescreen to cover the potential for a forthcoming defeat. His first election victory was a surprise for him and for the country, and months in advance of the next election he was constantly stoking the media coverage and communication with his base through tweets and rallies alleging that the 2020 election will be "rigged." Trump of course will blame the media regardless. This notable conspiracy theory tactic became a repetitive theme for tweets, shouts and critical comments about the media, and clearly established that Trump would stop at nothing to save face, place blame elsewhere and muddy the landscape with all manner of trash talk. Because of the multiple layers of voting oversight and differences in procedures state to state, most experts agree that rigging an election would be impossible; too many variables to even attempt to control. That said, this confidence does not address foreign influence on voters as they make their choices.

Trump's dependence on social media, Twitter most predominately, is remarkable. His inability to clearly communicate verbally is reinforced by the limitations of the platform and thus his profane rants take on even more importance for those who seek his latest wisdom that sets truth aside. The very real attraction for him is that he doesn't have to listen to anyone as he composes his epiphanies at all hours of the day and night, and the immediacy of hitting the send button on his phone is an addictive (power) behavior. In a published report from Pew Research Center there is a large component of Americans, 62 percent,[124] who get their news via social media platforms and many who depend on social media for their political news in particular, and more than half stated they have encountered made up news on these platforms. However, the Pew Research Center, through its standing American Trends Panel that consists of over 12,000 adults, provides some interesting additional insight. This group, consisting of both Democrats and Republicans in a survey panel in late 2019, expressed more distrust than trust of social media sites as sources for political and election news.[125] Further, those platforms most distrusted were Facebook, Instagram and yes, Twitter. To add another layer of data, that may or may not explain Trump's addiction to Twitter, 74 percent of Americans have little or no confidence in technology companies like Facebook, Twitter and Google to prevent the misuse of their platforms to influence voters for the 2020 presidential election.[126] Perhaps this lack of control is the attraction for Trump.

Isn't it interesting that when Twitter flagged two of Trump's tweets for fact-checking that he responded with a retaliatory executive order[127] with threats to shut down social media in one day? Compared to the months of inaction and absence of truthful statements regarding the pandemic, it is more than obvious that it is more important for this cancer to spread falsehoods than to be responsible and be accountable for the health of the nation. One day later as protests precipitated by the questionable police handling of an arrest and death of an African American in Minneapolis were becoming more violent and destructive, the Trump cancer pushed Twitter to the brink of its patience, particularly in light of a growing complaints about the inappropriateness of Trump tweets. The tweet in question posted by Trump was: "…These THUGS are dishonoring the memory of George Floyd[128], and I won't let that happen. Just spoke to Governor Tim Walz and told him that the Military is with him all the way. Any difficulty and we will assume control, but when the looting starts the shooting starts. Thank you!"[129] Within a few hours of Trump's early morning tweet, Twitter added a label warning to this tweet indicating that it violated a Twitter rule against glorifying violence.[130] In his habitual style, Trump attempted to convince Americans that he didn't know any history around the questionable "looting and shooting" verbiage in his tweet,[131] but denying his own statements in spite of all evidence to the contrary is routine behavior. If only, in the months leading up to the election and until the winner's inauguration in January 2021 that Twitter management would just shut down the platform in its entirety. Trumps primary megaphone with broad reach would no longer be available to him.

The Trump cancer tactical absurdities are certain to be the best possible examples of his orientation to "the likes of which we've never been seen before" and his use of absolute terms. Logic or intelligence does not easily apply to his remarks, or as one of his primary sources for topics and positions appearing in his tweets has stated, "I hate when people use my tactics against me."[132] As the protests that focused specifically on the death of George Floyd in Minneapolis on May 25 and more generally on actions against African Americans by local police forces as well as supporters of white supremacy, more cities around the country became the sites for peaceful elements of protest but unfortunately violence occurred predominantly in the forms of vandalism, looting and structural damage, even in Washington, DC, and in the vicinity of the White House. At one point the Secret Service moved Trump and family to the secure bunker in the White House per established procedure if there were ever a concern for their safety. Although denied by Trump to attempt to remove suspicion that the move was in any way because of his fear or imminent danger, he decided to portray the trip to the bunker as an inspection. Thus, after nearly four years in the White House it was time to inspect the bunker. Is there really a personal downside to being protected? There is something very wrong with this man.

Once again relying on outrageous and unhelpful tweets, the next day Trump subsequently boasted and made new threats in a series of tweets, but to what constructive purpose? Certainly not portraying leadership but more acting like an antagonist playground bully.

"Great job last night at the White House by the US @SecretService. They were not only totally professional, but very cool. I was inside, watched every move, and couldn't have felt more safe. They let the "protesters" scream & rant as much as they wanted, but whenever someone....

....got too frisky or out of line, they would quickly come down on them, hard - didn't know what hit them. The front line was replaced with fresh agents, like magic. Big crowd, professionally organized, but nobody came close to breaching the fence. If they had they would....

...have been greeted with the most vicious dogs, and most ominous weapons, I have ever seen. That's when people would have been badly hurt, at least. Many Secret Service agents just waiting for action. "We put the young ones on the front line, sir, they love it, and....

....good practice." As you saw last night, they were very cool & professional. Never let it get out of hand. Thank you! On the bad side, the D.C. Mayor @MurielBowser who is always looking for money and help wouldn't let the D.C. police get involved. Not their job. Nice!?"[132]

The tone of this tweet thread is appalling and to top it off he makes the subject political by attacking Mayor Bowser of the District of Columbia, a Democrat. To what end? The mayor's reaction: "I thought the president's remarks were gross, as I did when he said, 'if there's looting there will be shooting.' To make a reference to vicious dogs is now a subtle reminder to African Americans of segregationists who let dogs out on women, children and innocent people."[134] D.C. police coordinated with US Park Police and the Secret Service "throughout the evening and night, and at no time was [D.C. Police Chief Peter Newsham] concerned about losing control of protest activity in Washington, D.C."[135]

He doesn't understand, like most everything about the government, what the "rules of engagement" are with the various enforcement bodies, certainly around D.C. It is just so much easier to shoot from the hip, make unsubstantiated claims, inflame a situation beyond any semblance of necessity and of course make up his own rules and full steam ahead.

To counter the Trump "young ones" statement referencing specific agents, the Secret Service presented its own statement about what occurred with a post on Twitter:

"On Friday, May 29, and into early Saturday, May 30, 2020, US Secret Service Uniformed Division Officers made six arrests during demonstrations in and around Lafayette Park and along Pennsylvania Avenue near the White House.

Demonstrators repeatedly attempted to knock over security barriers on Pennsylvania Avenue. No individuals crossed the White House Fence and no Secret Service protectees were ever in any danger.

Some of the demonstrators were violent, assaulting Secret Service Officers and Special Agents with bricks, rocks, bottles, fireworks and other items. Multiple Secret Service Uniformed Division Officers and Special Agents sustained injuries from this violence.

The Secret Service respects the right to assemble, and we ask that individuals do so peacefully for the safety of all."[136]

What possible motive other than creating controversy by keeping his bizarre Twitter activity in front of the media and his base could Trump possibly have rationalized for such an easily provable series of false statements? As a tactic the Trump cancer succeeded. As a compassionate, informed and leader of the greatest country in the world, a dismal failure.

In what remains a controversial action while Trump was speaking (threatening) in the White House Rose Garden on June 1, action was taken against peaceful protesters to remove them from the Lafayette Square area near the White House, with some degree of direction apparently coming from Attorney General Barr. Numerous forces were involved including security officers, the Secret Service, military police, Park Police, District National Guard, and Arlington County, Virginia police involvement. Why? Trump decided a walk from the Rose Garden to St. John's Episcopal Church would make the stroll appear to be significant, but in reality this move created more controversy immediately in the moment and later as he posed for photographs in front of the church holding up a Bible that had been supplied to him. No speech, just a meaningless photo opportunity.

The Trump cancer is indeed a disease, proliferated by his ongoing irresponsible tactical elements employed that do not contribute to a remission of the disease, much less a cure that is only possible by his removal from office. The 2020 election is one means to facilitate that outcome, and prior to the election the 25th Amendment is another that might be precipitated by a total mental meltdown. That possibility is not out of the question considering behaviors that Trump exhibits. Either way, this disease could no longer directly wreak havoc on the country and Americans. He has been allowed by his own Party, and facilitators in the form of Republicans in fear of his potential negative impact on their careers, as they toss personal ethics aside as a mirror image of historic Trump. His administration "advisors" and his supporters have spent little or no time to understand what is happening to reduce the culture of the US to such a toxic environment. One would think that personal integrity would overrun such behavior.

If Trump is removed from office this won't bring a halt to his tweets and outlandish statements. He will find ways to salve his ego for the loss and removal as president and continue to be critical of individuals, institutions and the government to convince himself he was "robbed" of his destiny to be a second term president. Trump does not stand in the shadows thus he will be highly visible for an extended period, but hopefully for the country not too long. But what he hides that has the potential to be so impactful in so many ways concerns truth and trust. reflects his past. As president when you have no true values and only view the world with a binary view (I'm right you're wrong) the country will suffer.

The Trump cancer tactics have pervaded the country's institutions, its citizens and its relationships with allies. Trump has moved from attacks on everything that is wrong with the country as he launched his campaign for president in 2015 to an endless display of ignorance and egotism as president. He made unfounded charges against his Republican primary challengers. He used misogynistic rhetoric to attack his presidential election opponent and other women of strength. He has used deception, deceit and distractions as standard operating procedures. He has alienated democratic world leaders while embracing dictators. He has outwardly demonstrated his racism and xenophobia on many levels. He has exhibited his favoritism to all who praise him although that number is limited. He has used religion in a manipulative way, most notably as photo opportunities during a time of protests that quickly are condemned by religious leaders and others. He has exposed his overwhelming need to be viewed as powerful in the face of situations that call for decidedly more calm and reasonable responses. He has advocated for a show of force beyond any appropriate and humane need. He has continuously ignored the counsel of others whose experience and knowledge could help him, but that he most likely viewed as criticism when they did not blindly accept his opinion. He has shown an unmatched ability of mishandling crisis situations, most notably the health crisis that spread across this country and the world. He has shown no ability to truly manage people but instead just fires them if they disagree. Leadership, ethics and truth are striking deficits for this president.

America has been fooled. It is time to move on to recovery. Pope John Paul described the importance of a proper orientation to bring hope for a country long before Trump became a threat to civility and hope.

Love for one's country is thus a value to be fostered, without narrow-mindedness but with love for the whole human family and with an effort to avoid those pathological manifestations which occur when the sense of belonging turns into self-exaltation, the rejection of diversity, and forms of nationalism, racism and xenophobia.[137]

What Pope Paul identifies as pathological manifestations to be rejected make up the reality presented by Trump as president and Trump the man. Hope for the whole human family of America is severely threatened.

CHAPTER FIVE

Overcoming the Virus of the 45th Presidency

"The advancement and diffusion of knowledge is the only guardian of true liberty."

JAMES MADISON

It is time. No, it is way past time. After nearly four years of chaos, disruptions, misrepresentations and short-sided actions best described collectively as inciting division in the country, politicians, bureaucrats, scientists, medical professionals, world leaders and all Americans must recognize and voice the obvious. In the past many individuals previously silent have done just that. Trump is not stable. He is a destroyer of the principles upon which the country was founded and why it is respected. He does not represent the historic principles of the Republican Party. His behaviors demonstrate his patent lack of qualifications to be in any position of power, much less in the position as president of the US. His knowledge of government and governing is not just lacking, this knowledge and attribute is missing entirely.

He cannot get past his highest priority and that is a focus on himself, over all other significant areas of importance, including the well-being of all Americans. He is indeed the reality television "star" of his past but still ruminates over never being acknowledged with an Emmy. Is that of any importance to the rest of the world? Of course not, but not being "good enough" for an award he felt he deserved is representative of the Trump narcissist mindset and his orientation toward the world in general. I am the best, the smartest, the most successful, and oh yes, invincible, more than the world has ever seen before. The reality show that Trump has produced as president is dangerous for citizens, the country's future and the world.

In a characteristically absurd position Trump has even suggested the expertise of medical professionals, whose lives have been dedicated to medicine and infectious diseases in particular, is questionable and that what they have been recommending as the impact of the pandemic continues to grow is only a plot to damage him and his political standing prior to the 2020 election. Trump and others have taken the position that recommendations of true scientists and medical experts are just another "deep state" accusation toward these individuals who, unlike him, care about the health of Americans. It is so very appalling that anyone could think that such a conspiracy is being pursued just to damage him. Besides, such a plot is really not necessary as the Trump cancer does a wonderful job of consistently hurting himself. What is disturbingly obvious is that Trump did not have a plan with which to confront the pandemic. Instead he only reacted to anything that made his opinions irrelevant, incorrect or in some fashion actually required the government to act. Of even greater concern is that he turned the pandemic into an extremely biased political maneuver over scientific discovery, innovation and management. Many in the Trump inner circle seem to facilitate this position at every turn where another term of office, and perhaps their own job security, is more important than the growing number of American fatalities.

Trump just doesn't listen to many true advisers, with the intelligence community constituting a prime example. When exposed to information of importance it has been reported by White House sources, from those who have left the administration, those still on staff and those present in meetings, that he has a concentration span that goes far beyond the accepted criteria for attention deficit disorder for a child, or an adult. From the beginning of his presidency it was reported that Trump didn't read or study and thus any hope of him developing an opinion, much less a policy, based on fact, history, intelligence or the counsel of others is quite impossible to imagine. The alternative facts he prefers to use always circle back to his greater knowledge as the Oz of his personal alternative universe. His outwardly displayed mental capacity is a target-rich environment for criticism. He has great difficulty putting together even a short cohesive sentence that communicates a cognizant point. Instead he combines words and topics that are unrelated but always injects many of his favorite false claims and criticisms directed toward those who disagree with him; media reporting, individuals he has fired, world leaders, opposition party leaders, past administration leadership (both Parties), and true experts he chooses to contradict with his stable genius mental acuity. It's like trying to capture a fly buzzing around your kitchen that never lands. The Trump cancer is so multifaceted that the presenting cancerous symptoms cannot be fully detailed, but those most apparent unquestionably provide sufficient information for a diagnosis many suspect and others deny.

In the political arena standing up to the absurdities of the Trump cancer is not difficult, assuming of course that individuals are comfortable with the unequivocal fact that they are destined to become targets of a Trump attack. Republicans in the legislative branch are excellent examples of those who fear his wrath. An illustration of note is when Trump decided to visit the Ford Motor Company during the growing threat of the Covid-19 pandemic. It was a political move of course to billboard his persuasion skills in encouraging the company to become involved in producing needed respiratory ventilators. The need was real and notably exacerbated during the Trump-induced delayed buildup of needed equipment identified earlier in the year as the pandemic was spreading across the country. In reality his visit was a pathetic political maneuver to gain media coverage. (Look'ee here, see what I brought you…me!) But as was his visible habit in public, there was no reason to expect that he would not continue to ignore all manner of guidelines regarding virus mitigation steps.

Trump had gone on record stating that wearing a mask while sitting in the Oval Office was not for him, and he also had routinely ignored wearing a mask in public even when reasonable caution would dictate otherwise. Even before the pandemic masks were commonplace in healthcare settings, when manufacturing of products produced toxic fumes and even with some routine service industry employees. Historically masks had a negative image as they were part of the uniform of robbers and burglars. As he robs America of its healthcare, responsible governing and absence of ethical behavior as president, he doesn't need to hide behind a mask as the forementioned burglar would do. His "steals" are out in the open for all to see. Prior to his Ford Motor Company visit the attorney general of Michigan made the president and the White House aware of the state's policy regarding the wearing of masks that was in place: "Anyone who has potentially been recently exposed, including the President of the United States has not only a legal responsibility, but also a social and moral responsibility to take reasonable precautions to prevent further spread of the virus."[138] In Michigan this was also a state law by virtue of the governor's executive order. Ford also shared its factory protocol regarding the wearing of masks in advance of Trump's visit.

It was confirmed after this Ford visit that for a short time in a small area of the factory with no media present, that Trump did indeed wear a mask.[139] But when it came time for a more visible photo opp at Ford with the media present, he did not wear a mask. This was his standard procedure throughout the growth of Covid-19 cases and deaths as some sort of a personal rebellion against the guidelines of the White House and the CDC. Michigan Attorney General Nessel was quick to criticize the president's lack of compliance and stated, "The president is like a petulant child who refuses to follow rules." The Trump response: "The Wacky Do Nothing Attorney General of Michigan, Dana Nessel, is viciously threatening Ford Motor Company for the fact that I inspected a Ventilator plant without a mask. Not their fault, and I did put on a mask."[140] Not exactly a quality response through which to prove a "petulant child" reference wrong is it? And of course, his statement is classic Trump hair-splitting as he wore a mask in one area but in the larger plant area in front of a considerable gathering of people and cameras, he didn't. More to the point, Ford did not execute its own mitigation policy with Trump nor adhere to the governor's executive order. When Ford's executive chairman, William Ford Jr., was asked "can you confirm the president was told it is OK not to wear a mask in this area," Ford shrugged and said, "It's up to him![141]

"The Lamestream Media is doing everything within their power to foment hatred and anarchy. As long as everybody understands what they are doing, that they are FAKE NEWS and truly bad people with a sick agenda, we can easily work through them to GREATNESS!"[142] This particular tweet could be a type of reverse communication as he is accusing the media of inciting hatred and anarchy when in reality this is his standard approach in addressing his base of supporters, particularly in his demeaning, accusatory and hate-filled rants at his rallies. Interesting isn't it? Fake news that he can't seem to live without.

He craves media attention but loathes it when he gets it and then attacks, *e.g.*, "the enemy of the people." Does this child have a justifiable sandbox to play in? Is a free press an enemy of the people or just Trump's personal bogeyman under his bed? The significance of this child at work at Ford, with all possible grace applied, begs the question of what possible positive message does his behavior send to the public at-large with people understandably concerned about their health, and more specifically to the people of Michigan whose state at that point had experienced 53,009 positive cases of the coronavirus and 5,060 deaths?[143]

But, as part of continuing evidence that every action is about Trump's desire to accept no responsibility even in a situation where some level of Covid-19 mitigation steps may be implemented, control is difficult. Determined to entertain his base in the midst of the pandemic remaining a major concern around the country, he added the following to an Internet pre-registration request for tickets for his first rally redux in Tulsa, Oklahoma.

"By clicking register below, you are acknowledging that an inherent risk of exposure to COVID-19 exists in any public place where people are present," the statement reads. By attending the Rally, you and any guests voluntarily assume all risks related to exposure to COVID-19 and agree not to hold Donald J. Trump for President, Inc.; BOK Center; ASM Global; or any of their affiliates, directors, officers, employees, agents, contractors, or volunteers liable for any illness or injury."[144]

After exercising his mismanagement expertise in terms of public health, he still focuses on a CYA[145] for himself. It gets better. In the face of protests across the country, and across from the White House, following the murder of George Floyd, the Trump cancer demonstrated his lack of compassion and humanity by selecting the date for the rally as June 19th, the date of an organized killing of blacks in Tulsa in 1921 that became known as Juneteenth, a day of emancipation recognition.

Even though the administration later stated it was aware of the significance of the date, the rally was scheduled anyway. But later, after objections were raised in the Tulsa black community specifically, from the Black Lives Matter (BLM) movement and complaints registered from around the country, the rally was postponed until the next day, June 20th. The Trump tweet stated that he was honoring the requests of others to not hold the rally on Juneteenth, not acknowledging his or his administration's blatant amateurish mistake in the first place; there's that no accountability/responsibility gene popping up again. The Trump cancer's lack of sensitivity to an active and significant additional crisis situation griping the country as a whole, around the treatment of blacks and systemic racism, police brutality, and controversies around the involvement of Trump himself in the protests was quite remarkable. His remarks were frequently the equivalent of throwing a chemical accelerant on an open flame.

Most of his statements during the period of the protests taking place in cities from coast to coast were inflammatory, divisive and irresponsible. In an American Trends Panel survey published June

12, 2020 findings included that 48 percent of adults generally and 68 percent of black adults specifically felt that Trump has made race relations worse.[146] This is in stark contrast to Trump's oft-repeated claim of "doing more for blacks that any other president." To accept this claim, one would have to also accept his frequent racist statements, his attacks on voting rights that primarily positively benefit minorities and his false boasts of saving historic black colleges and universities even though funding came through Congress. In spite of him wanting to make an association with a favorable economy prior to the pandemic impact, black unemployment and poverty rates had been declining long before he took office. Reality or fantasy it just doesn't matter to the Trump cancer. Whatever will generate a headline that is easily repeated by himself and by his base is his motivation, with truth not a required criterion.

The Trump cancer is surrounded with a large group of excuse makers and spinmeisters and exhibiting remarkable bench strength as they all are experienced players. With great frequency they must get in the game to try to recover from the cancer's tweets, uninformed opinions, off-handed comments and more. Many of this group of facilitators have no hesitation to create their own lies and false claims and speak far beyond their areas of expertise. Controlling the uncontrollable is a difficult assignment and the president generates a dangerous, and most often, unplanned daily agenda. Television is the Trump cancer's "executive time" source library, seeking out those who agree with him and criticizing those who don't. Trump's addition to social media, with Twitter leading the way, has also precipitated issues. At the time of his election his Party in its platform chose to criticize President Obama in the following way. "The survival of the Internet as we know it is at risk. Its gravest peril originates in the White House, the current occupant of which has launched a campaign, both at home and internationally, to subjugate it to agents of government."[147] The Republican Party had no idea what was coming from Trump.

The "peril to the Internet" grows each day as this disease shows no signs of lessening its negativity on the country through outrageous tweets online. During the early months of the administration's bungled management of the pandemic Trump's bizarre statements and logic were on full display. With each briefing from Trump the Task Force numbers were thrown around like peanuts at a circus. Masks, ventilators, swabs, or tests were all about numbers, but containment of the virus and science was an afterthought at best or left to others to go on record. The Trump cancer imparted information through its own unique language. Clarity was not the objective and true facts were generally lacking as double-speak prevailed. Trump wanted to present himself as being the authority at all times and the following is a representative example. "When you test, you have a case. When you test, you find something is wrong with people. If we didn't do any testing, we would have very few cases."[148] This particular position was repeated ad infinitum for months as evidence of Trump's "ignore it and it will go away" strategy. Conclusion: he wasn't really interested in the health of Americans. And a week later as he tried to describe his own most recent experience of being tested for Covid-19 he propounded, "…and I tested very positively in another sense. This morning. Yeah, I tested positively toward negative, right? So I tested perfectly this morning. Meaning I tested negative."[149] Well, that clears that up.

Facing any situation when an ability to communicate is markedly impaired presents many issues. Add to that a non-negotiable attitude towards being open to alternative points of view and all the ingredients exist for a recipe for disastrous dialogue. If the Trump cancer's deep-seated temperamental traits were to be genuinely evaluated by a multi-specialty medical professional assessment, including psychiatrists and psychologists, the variety of diagnostic criteria that he would meet hands down for several severe personality disorders would be quite revealing.[150] Cognitively he exhibits consistent episodes of an inability to speak clear thoughts as his brain is in a state of gymnastics leaping from point to point, but never sticking a landing. What is deeper rooted are his potentially uncontrollable reasons for performing the way he does.

America has unfortunately inherited all of the shortcomings and attacks levied by the Trump cancer. The disease has taken its toll. America needs a cure that will halt the spread of chaos over the lives of its citizens. On occasion Trump expresses optimism, usually about something he wants to take credit for, but in very short order he follows those statements with pessimism and/or criticism of someone or some group and in effect takes what might be a positive moment and turns it to a negative. Medically cancer is determined to wreak havoc if not destroy the body entirely and end a life without discrimination as to the patient's age, gender, heritage or other defining characteristics. The Trump cancer is also oriented to wreak havoc with the same lack of caring, but he portrays this behavior as winning. It's always about winning, for himself. But when Trump says he wins Americans must ask themselves "what have I lost." Initially, as he rode down the Trump Tower escalator to announce his candidacy in 2015, Trump was viewed as an egotistical joke. He had all sorts of baggage surrounding him from his various enterprises, and his historic preferred resolution tactics for any problem were lawsuits; break down the opposition to the point they will just walk away. But Americans can't walk away from the Trump cancer's actions as president. The impact is immediate and far reaching, and the country will suffer long after the country benefits from a different type of remission as the cancer vacates the Oval Office.

Even before that fateful escalator moment in New York City there were clues to what was ahead for the country. "My IQ is one of the highest and you all know it! Please don't feel so stupid or insecure; It's not your fault."[151] Today many still laugh but there is nothing humorous about the undesirable bearing he has had on the country, programs of importance that have global impact and deterioration of important relationships with allies. Laughing at his continual irrational behavior and fact checking his shocking statements doesn't address the country's needs. Fact checking is a routine procedure for professional journalists but with Trump fact checking has become a career path for many. Consider what is wrong with him, intellectually, morally and ethically and stir in his exploits and the conclusion is undeniable. The Trump cancer must be excised in some manner and no longer allowed to advance its destructive ways on the country and around the world. No amount of partisanship behavior, rally support and cheerleading based on emotion and bravado instead of facts and truth can possibly provide a pathway for success for the country.

"Once a country is habituated to liars,
it takes generations to get the truth back."

———— GORE VIDAL ————

There is no argument to dispute or alter Trump's documented propensity to lie. Speeches written by others that in some instances clearly illustrate the writer's own biased agendas are read unemotionally by Trump. He stumbles through them and is frequently bewildered by words he isn't comfortable pronouncing. Perhaps he does not even possess an understanding of their meaning. But it's fairly obvious that whatever input he may have had in preparing his remarks, his true thoughts ring out when he strays from the prompter as he compliments himself and makes unsubstantiated and embellished claims. These unchecked exaggerations will frequently establish a position that surprises his staff, make Republicans in general scratch their heads in wonderment or just contribute to their embarrassment in some way. Countless hours are employed by the West Wing staff, Cabinet members, Republican senators, Fox News etc., to confront and correct the Trump cancer's countless hours spent generating false claims and lies, gaffes and out-of-control tweets. It makes one wonder if the country truly has a president accountable to citizens, or someone just playing a role when not swinging a golf club. No Emmy coming his way for this performance either.

But one thing for certain, whether recovery begins if he leaves office in January 2021, or four years later, it will indeed "take generations to get the truth back" and overcome the "American carnage" that the Trump cancer proclaimed would end as he made his January 20, 2017 inaugural address. Instead, the carnage has grown to unimaginable proportions during his time in office and his slaughter of American ideals and institutions has created another kind of American pandemic that he can claim is all his own.

CHAPTER SIX

Authenticity and Transparency Essential for Remission

"People think that a liar gains a victory over his victim. What I've learned is that a lie is an act of self-abdication, because one surrenders one's reality to the person to whom one lies, making that person one's master, condemning oneself from then on to faking the sort of reality that person's view requires to be faked...
The man who lies to the world, is the world's slave from then on...
There are no white lies, there is only the blackest of destruction and a white lie is the blackest of all."[152]

AYN RAND

The Ayn Rand quote above is worth a thought-by-thought unpacking to understand its application to the Trump cancer.

"People think that a liar gains a victory over his victim."

It is well-documented that Trump's daily modus operandi is to use lies as distractions and to deflect a direct confrontation when his fragmented knowledge and lack of competence betrays rational thought. He may indeed view his behavior as victorious as at all times he wants to appear to be immune to any challenge. Appearance is one thing, but reality is something quite different. If anyone is listening the only possible first thought is how can he say that? It's not true. Does he think all Americans are fools? Well, to this latter question the answer is yes, if he feels he can use anyone or any group to a perceived advantage.

"What I've learned is that a lie is an act of self-abdication, because one surrenders one's reality to the person to whom one lies, making that person one's master, condemning oneself from then on to faking the sort of reality that person's view requires to be faked..."

First point: there is no possibility that Trump would ever give away his perception of his power through a lie or other means to anyone. A bully will always default to anger and lies to build up his strength in his own eyes. Second point: Trump gives the appearance that he does become trapped into continuing to foster a lie, usually with another lie or at minimum a repetitiveness of words that are confounding to most reasonable people.

"There are no white lies, there is only the blackest of destruction and a white lie is the blackest of all."

To be fair, little white lies come easily from Trump's mouth. It is a natural occurrence and may be his most highly developed skill. However, Americans, and others, are forced into a reluctant acceptance that some of what he may feel are white lies, planned or unplanned, are far more than that and are indeed bold and dark in their potential for tragic outcomes. The Trump cancer attacks through lies. No person, concept or fact is immune to his vile approach to the world and all become targets with no regard for who or what is damaged along the way.

The Trump cancer that is seen and heard is not disguised. By definition Trump is indeed authentic, what you see is what you get, but not the authenticity that is expected of the president of the US. Trump communications, whatever method they may use, are rarely if ever authentic. To be considered authentic what is being said or written needs to be reliable because the information would be based on facts, not emotion or ego. If this simple formula were followed there would be a much higher bar set for believability. And if the information was more believable, and minus the political rhetoric and obstruction, progress on multiple levels may well result. But the reality of Trump and his administration's communications is something far less. They range from completely incoherent rants, unsubstantiated attacks on institutions and individuals and in many instances reflect an unmitigated stonewalling of truth and defiance of the rule of law.

To determine if statements have some basis in fact is relatively easy as the Trump cancer's megaphone delivery normally makes it clear. He searches desperately for words particularly when his knowledge of the topic is grossly insufficient or when he wants to portray an image of authority and power. Any spontaneous comment is seldom authentic, and words are delivered in a very halting fashion when read from a teleprompter and are clearly not Trump's own. His delivery is so deficient that it is quite easy for those he is addressing to not listen at all. No sincerity, empathy or introduction of confidence is imparted to the listener. Extemporaneous speaking is not a strong suit. The words flow but communication is lacking. A common occurrence is listening for his next mistake, lie or misspeak instead of any content of substance. On the occasion when he likes something, he just heard himself say, he will frequently seek to embellish the point by repeating words and adding to them but rarely adding meaningful detail nor portraying strategic or critical thinking. At one time when making reference to Puerto Rico in the aftermath of Hurricane Maria, "this is an island surrounded by water, big water, ocean water."[153] At the time of this speech some felt this was a milestone and an authentic moment for Trump as at least on this occasion he demonstrated he could grasp true facts and his statement was believable, and true.

Moving on, for Trump to exhibit full and responsible transparency a commitment would need to be made to not intentionally hide anything, *i.e.*, no secrets, but information that needed to be communicated to the American people. If an individual is perceived as not being transparent the downside is fairly significant in terms of an inability to make positive contributions to support a strategic agenda. The management/leadership goal should be to not provide reasons for anyone to have suspicions or other concerns about what is being said or shown in some way. There is no doubt that for anyone who is in a position of protecting national security in a variety of ways or facing a situation where exposing information may jeopardize an outcome such as in a time of military conflict, revealing sensitive information could be harmful. As president of the US striking a balance or making communication decisions on a daily basis to instill confidence in Americans, makes transparency essential to introducing confidence. Being transparent signals honesty, not just as a desirable concept but in actual evidence that it exists. If indeed that evidence is present trust is a potential and highly desirable outcome.

The Trump cancer has done little to display honesty through words or actions nor have many of those around him, so trust is not a commodity distinctly present either. Being transparent does have downside as if even unintentionally it will expose truth and lies. Having an expectation that a president would indeed be transparent is not a leap of faith that is difficult to accept. Unfortunately, the Trump cancer has obliterated this possibility and the country has suffered immensely. Trump has only displayed *cri de coeur*, complaining, criticizing and fearmongering about anything that is not his idea and protesting against all who do not provide the support he demands. Infinitely the Trump cancer practices what he commented to journalist Bob Woodward during an interview in 2016. "Real power is, I don't even want to use the word, fear."[154]

Although difficult to quantify, fear is an ally of cancer in the body and can negatively impact whatever resistance an individual can bring to bear against the disease. Trump promotes fear with every derogatory remark, threat and overpromise he makes in an effort to gain support, with the inference that if that support isn't given the wrath of Trump will prevail, or the Democrats will ruin your lives forever. At one point during the period of primary campaigning the Trump cancer vowed "don't worry, we'll take the country back,"[155] with a heavy focus on anti-immigration, losing jobs to China and most any other association he could make to invoke fear in the minds of his audience. The Trump cancer has fears of its own, with the independence of the Federal Bureau of Investigation (FBI) being an organization at the top of the list. He can fire directors and others in the organization but what he cannot do is control the dedication of what Bureau employees are committed to each and every day.

The Trump cancer rebels at others briefing him by rejecting truth, advice and counsel. The infamous movie dialogue of "you can't handle the truth"[156] is remarkably apropos for Trump. He just can't handle it. He goes so far off the rails that he can't recognize truth. It's as if truth is threatening to him and thus authenticity and transparency are quite impossible. Instead Trump makes unfounded statements and threats without proof of any type to support them, broadly uses absolute terms as notable exaggerations, and subsequently his press secretary will try to spin support or a form of positive interpretation but rarely do these attempts create credibility. Trump will frequently circle back then deny the "corrections" coming from others and this creates more melodrama that perhaps is entertainment for him but just plain denial for all others. For all of his spontaneous remarks that most likely are prejudiced reactions rather than a reflection of some well thought out strategy, Trump brings consistent disgrace on his presidency and the country.

The great dealmaker cut a deal with himself at the time of the threat of a coronavirus pandemic was revealed to the public in January 2020 base perhaps in the form of "how can I use this?" The deal the cancerous Trump presidency struck against Americans is one best described as absolution, "ignore it and it will go away." It is as if he took the position that "if I don't acknowledge it, people won't notice." It's the Trump equivalent of a child's fear. "If I don't think about the bogyman under the bed he isn't really there." The Trump cancer addiction to numbers, even if not understood, continuously propels him into a mode of underestimating the pandemic's threat to Americans or overstating any number that he assumes will be beneficial to him. As was normal behavior for Trump he apparently saw the potential looming healthcare crisis as a spotlight moment to do something big that will make him appear powerful. It didn't matter that he had little confirmed details with which to work with at that time, but he was not interested in epidemiological models or the expertise of scientists and science in general. It didn't matter. It never mattered. He flailed his hands and attempted to make statements that showed his superior knowledge. Yet from the earliest moments of his awareness of what had originated in China it was all he needed, or wanted, to know. Look out world, I'm the expert and I'm in charge. There was nothing authentic or transparent about his ignorance and cancerous approach to the problem. Perhaps he was considering yet another wall, but what was revealed later[11] was that he did indeed know much more and wasn't being transparent.

Remember that the House of Representatives identified the cancer and had voted to impeach Trump on December 18, 2019, and coincidentally at this point on the calendar concern about Covid-19 was heating up around the world. He was also facing his impeachment trial in the Senate after the first of the year. It had long been established that focusing on two things at once was always a challenge for Trump. In this case, the trial was certainly personal and another opportunity to yell hoax and fraud in the direction of the Democrats. The ultimate outcome of the impeachment proceedings could have had far-reaching implications for the remainder of his first term in office as well as what it could mean for his reelection. He certainly had the opportunity to pull a Nixon and resign but the Trump inner demons and personality would never consider that route.

Remembering that Trump had made VP Pence the chair of the White House Task Force on the pandemic one would think that if only by associative osmosis he would had understood what medical experts have been describing to him over an extended period of time. After all, he was always in "the room where it happens"[157] but there was no guarantee he was listening. In yet another example of irresponsible commentary, in June 2020 Pence offered the following as the coronavirus was taking a much stronger foothold in the US. "In recent days, the media has taken to sounding the alarm bells over a 'second wave' of coronavirus infections. Such panic is overblown. Thanks to the leadership of President Trump and the courage and compassion of the American people, our public health system is far stronger than it was four months ago, and we are winning the fight against the invisible enemy."[158] The Trump cancer had undoubtedly invaded Pence beginning from their earliest conversations regarding his selection for the election ticket in 2016. Maybe for Pence it was about a different election, 2024 perhaps, but with continuing events why would the country want to impose another crisis upon itself?

When he arose each morning Pence's only role at each public appearance seemed to be to compliment the president and make overwhelmingly inaccurate statements about Trump's outstanding leadership. His comments were authentic for him in terms of mirroring the president's false statements. That much was transparent. The Trump cancer's concurrent malignant strain in the form of the vice president did not seem to want to be helpful but instead was only concerned with stroking the ego of the boss. Being concerned about a second wave of the virus or even a continuing period of the first wave had absolutely nothing to do with the partial recovery of the public health system or winning any fight. The administration's response remained poorly lacking and Pence's awareness of the knowledge Trump has subsequently early in 2020 has not been confirmed, but if he was aware then he was complicit in the withholding of that information.

And certainly, it was not about the media sounding an alarm bell and having some sort of ulterior motive. The media was responsibly reporting expert opinions without any political motives, unlike what was coming from the administration. Those on the front lines of managing Covid-19 cases including researchers and epidemiologists studying what was occurring, medical providers and victims and their families certainly didn't see it that way, and were appreciative of the media taking responsibility for attempting to provide authentic and accurate information from the White House. For all of these folks the outlook for the future was daunting and they were sounding the warnings, not the media. The administration's messaging was confusing and at times contradictory and its ulterior motive was about building a platform, as shaky as it might be, about the economy and the looming election. Encouraging states to lift restrictions so that Trump may be able to talk about the economy in a positive fashion appeared to be the focus. The messaging was not helpful. Topics such as millions of tests being available but reducing the actual testing was confusing at best, the importance of contact tracing was not loudly supported and issues relating to states getting access to necessary materials was creating a fertile environment for more Covid-19 cases. Not delivering important messages to the public was just irresponsible as the Trump administration was resembling an ostrich with its head buried in the sand. They were not acting with transparency or authenticity even as hard as the science experts were trying to right the ship.

There are Americans who looked to Trump for information that could be trusted and in some way be comforting. This is not an unusual orientation or wish from any president, but Trump is far unlike most presidents. Results from a Pew Internet Research survey published at the end of May,[159] indicated that Americans who relied most on Trump and the Task Force for information about Covid-19 are looking for information about the economic downside of the pandemic (60 percent) and how the federal government is responding (49 percent). Transparent answers to these information needs were lacking as most content from Trump was critical of either the states or the Democrats or both. Further, 51 percent of those who rely most on Trump and the Task Force say the outbreak has been exaggerated, compared with just eight percent who say it's been deemphasized too much. It would be interesting to survey this same group again as the number of positive US cases has risen to over 7 million, and deaths from the virus total over 200,000.[160] Exaggerated? Really?

Trump has a negative orientation to the world and everything around him. Because he assumes the mantra of always being right, everyone else must, by his default, be wrong. It is quite possible that his first reaction to most any topic, decision or solution begins with negative thinking. "All those before me were losers." "It's never been done that way." "Fake news." On the other hand, what he speaks and tweets that he would profess are positive statements would not pass a smell test for accuracy, ever. It's all or nothing with Trump; his way, his thoughts, his perceptions are what count. He is so adept at making unproven and false generalizations that almost anything he believes as being negative, including someone not exhibiting total loyalty to him or expressing opinions critical of him in some way, he then proceeds to what he feels are the most productive conclusions for him. For example, he must believe that labeling someone with a derogatory nickname gives him power over them or communicates to others that he is afraid of no one. Another power tactic is blaming others for interfering with him in some way and one small questionable detail or made up situation becomes his focus to the point of its endless repetition, *e.g.*, reliving some aspect of the 2016 election or his opponent.

Perhaps a little pass/fail coaching is in order:

Keep your thoughts positive because your thoughts become your words.
Keep your words positive because your words become your behavior.
Keep your behavior positive because your behavior becomes your habits.
Keep your habits positive because your habits become your values.
Keep your values positive because your values become your destiny.

——————————— MAHATMA GANDHI ———————————

There is no question that his thoughts do become his words, though positivity is consistently lacking and more frequently just his brand of gamesmanship. His words are patently negative as is his behavior. His bad behavior is decidedly a habit of grand proportions, and there is no question his habits of all varieties reflect whatever values he sees as valuable, and his destiny therefore is negative. One of the Trump cancer's habits is to make threats, veiled or direct. One day prior to his first campaign rally in Tulsa, Oklahoma following the pandemic lockdown and BLM[161] protests across the country Trump decided his best advance presidential moment would be to threaten non-specific harsh action. "Any protesters, anarchists, agitators, looters or lowlifes who are going to Oklahoma please understand, you will not be treated like you have been in New York, Seattle or Minneapolis. It will be a much different scene!"[162] This statement is a fair representation of his thoughts, words, behaviors, habits and values that assure his destructive, harmful and negative legacy.

It is quite impossible to be authentic or transparent when the first thought, the first reaction and the first action take the combined form of denying facts. Words previously spoken or tweeted, change the subject or in some other convoluted way intending to distract. Far more disturbing is the fact that these things come from the president of the US. By creating a situation that may be even more outrageous, disruptive and offensive to many creates a sense of astonishment and dread for sane individuals trying to discern what is driving such bizarre behavior. It's a WWE-style mental wrestling match on display. The common denominator in this equation is that it seems as if the Trump cancer bases all of his obsessions on lies and his perceived invincibility. The subject doesn't matter. The needs of Americans don't matter. A total lack of preparedness doesn't matter. An illogical presentation of Trump facts is all that is important. As president, Trump has access to excessive amounts of information, insights and experience that is difficult to quantify. Instead he is apparently educated on a daily basis, and at night, by some Fox News anchors with their inbred bias. It has not been difficult to trace some tweet content to something said by a Fox employee who possesses similar uninformed insights. On most every day, or night, the words and positions Trump takes for his tweets, answers to media questions or interactions with those in the administration range from a consistent theme of racist commentary voiced through his self-constructed superior persona, to what appears to be a singular orientation to creating controversy.

The fact that white supremacist, racist and anti-immigrant rants come from within the White House and are not limited to Trump's tweets and media responses, because negative and inflammatory viewpoints find their way into formal remarks prepared for him by others whose views are well documented. The cracks in the Trump cancer's Twitter armor appear through tweets quite obviously carefully crafted by others that reveal organized thought, grammar, spelling expertise and actually communicate a point, but nevertheless are representative of Trump's disparaging themes and those that come from the work of others. They are just polished up a bit in their delivery. The disquieting consistency however is that the rhetoric is misleading, inaccurate and most often constructed from some alternative fantasy world.

In a country founded on the rule of law as the ultimate bar to be met in all matters, a US president's duty is above all else to adhere to and defend the Constitution. Sadly, offensively, this is not where the country finds itself today. The Trump cancer touts the Constitution in one misplaced statement after another, but even if Trump has read it (highly speculative of course) he only wants to focus on the power that he thinks it provides him personally, not the presidency and not the people. Those he has chosen to accuse of treason need not fear as he has no understanding of what constitutes such a charge. "Whoever, owing allegiance to the United States, levies war against them or adheres to their enemies, giving them aid and comfort within the United States or elsewhere, is guilty of treason and shall suffer death, or shall be imprisoned not less than five years and fined under this title but not less than $10,000; and shall be incapable of holding any office under the United States."[163] Trump throwing out an accusation towards individuals, newspapers and other entities with no substance or the slightest element of truth. No one has levied war against the US and other than suspicions about himself and others in his administration, no one has given aid and comfort to an enemy, at least what is known. The problem with his approach is that what he thinks he is empowered to do he grossly misunderstands, overstates or just assumes and makes things up that are not in or even implied by the Constitution or US Code. Authentic? Yet more examples of how the word does not apply to this man as president.

Trump routinely makes statements that are offensive to one or more groups in American society and others around the world. But registering offense toward individuals or governments doesn't seem to really matter to Trump. He speaks as if he represents a fascist state, not a democracy. He is indifferent, or perhaps more directly, unconcerned about the rights of others. The Trump cancer has also shown that he is on both sides of the equation when it comes to violence. On the one hand he will incite violence through his uncontrolled statements, yet will quickly condemn violence, particularly if he feels it will work to his advantage over one demographic group or another. Cancer in the body doesn't withhold a particular hesitation to where it attacks. It adapts and it lies. It's game on with any organ or body system it can invade. The Trump cancer too doesn't discriminate. Everyone and everything are targets. If one took the time to undertake a true textual analysis of Trump's rhetoric, the depth of his contradictions, vile comments and inappropriate criticisms it would undoubtedly handily reinforce the degree to which Trump is unprepared to be in office. Twitter in particular is his favorite platform. He uses his thumbs to stab out letters to send posts on Twitter reflecting his demented feelings and what he wants, unencumbered by the editing of others as he posts during late night and early morning hours from his residence in the White House, or wherever in the world he may be. In a recent permanent suspension of a comedian who made transphobic remarks in his use of the platform, Twitter stated that the individual "...has been permanently suspended after repeated violations of our rules against hateful conduct and platform manipulation." If this is a true statement, it's fairly obvious that the Trump cancer receives a pass of sorts each and every day. Twitter of late has flagged some of his tweets, notably some that were made nearly inciting violence and threatening retaliation as protests were taking place.

Trump, and others in his sphere, continuously make reference to the Resolute desk in the Oval Office. Why? The significance of that desk, its origin, historical moments and true accomplishments in its presence for many presidents is lost with Trump. For this reality president it is just a prop, with Pence the ever-present guard standing behind him against a rear attack, and the desk is one more misrepresented object in the Trump toy box. It's almost as if he thinks that sitting behind that desk allows him to command respect when in reality the acts he takes and oversees from that desk results in just the opposite view. A pompous attitude and consistent condescending language don't command respect. It is quite impossible for anyone to be the person Trump believes himself to be and tries to sell himself to others. Trump is more suited to be a dictator of a small country situated on an island (surrounded by big water!), and isolated from the rest of the world. Even in this scenario the inhabitants of this country would steadily be heading for their boats.

Cancer has no protocol, no prescribed leadership behavior pattern or in any way is expected to act in a certain way with every individual. Trump ignores protocol in routine interactions with those who deserve his recognition and respect. He instead believes, and says, that even leaders of other countries do not know what they are doing, and they need to follow his advice. He believes this without reservation but what he doesn't understand, or frankly doesn't care about, is the world's disappointment with him as a leader, particularly his handling of the pandemic in the US, much less his behavior in a presidential election debate. It's only adoration he wants. Trust, truth and authenticity are not present. Transparency into his motivations, however, are very much apparent. The Trump cancer plays with people. Sarcasm, winks and expletives mask (no, not that one), or so Trump believes, the incompetence toward which the office is approached and mismanaged. Trump personifies the phrase of suffering from a bad case of lack of common sense as he seems incapable of understanding the pain he is perpetrating on the country. He only sees success as he defines it, infrequently real but definitely imagined in his mind.

*"I refuse to accept the view that mankind is so tragically bound to the starless midnight of racism and war that the bright daybreak of peace and brotherhood can never become a reality...
I believe that unarmed truth and unconditional love will have the final word."*

——————— MARTIN LUTHER KING, JR. ———————

There is such a cloud of deception enveloping the Trump White House that more time is committed to lying about the lies than working and honestly speaking needed and powerful truth to the American people. Each day features the calamity of the moment with little to no positive outcome for the country. Through the years since the Trump cancer has infected the lives of Americans and scorched the values that are most sacred to the morale of the country, the horizon for responsible leadership is obscured and instead there is no truth or leadership at all coming from the Oval Office. There is so much false history and deceit presented by Trump that each statement he makes is subject to questions about intent, rationale and at times even his sanity. He thinks he is showing strength, "greater than ever before," that he is in total control, "I read everything" (all evidence to the contrary), and in the depths of his clattered mind he truly believes he is always right, "I know a lot." The most meaningful yet basic questions remain, however, and these are does he know the difference between right and wrong and does he really care about the country or just himself? Every passing day the answers to both questions are reinforced. Always right, and no.

He catches his own staff and cabinet off guard by agreeing to one position only to make statements later that unscramble the egg he has previously cooked and discount previous conclusions that may have already been acted upon. From the press secretary and up and down the organization chart people are scrambling for answers and responses that make the president look as if he is the "genius" he professes to be, while being as careful as possible that their bobbing and weaving responses don't totally and negatively reflect on them and their own ongoing credibility. Well, some of these people anyway. On neither front is this possible as there are many who have suffered while being loyal, and others who have left the administration because they had had enough of the environment in general and some who were told that they weren't loyal enough. Trump has shown that his lack of transparency with those who are attempting to help him, even if their own beliefs may differ, makes for a distasteful lack of confidence in the president.

In a time of any real crisis situation, ordering a KFC lunch or retracting a mulligan on the golf course ("I didn't say that") the Trump cancer shows no tendency at all to let facts get in the way, ever. He prefers to challenge the media at all times when his misbehavior, past and present, is reported that he consistently refers to as fake news. A situation reported that perhaps hits too close to home is characterized as a hoax. It is quite a remarkable condition he attempts to create with those who believe his every word. It's really the Trump cancer version of using a process described in Aldous Huxley's classic book, *Brave New World*, called hypnopaedia, a mental conditioning practice based on the repetition of selected phrases over and over again.[19] This may be a reasonable explanation for the steadfast support of many of his base of supporters, and the applause Trump encourages when he uses the fake news and hoax descriptors with unwavering frequency at his rallies. Did Trump proactively research this process, not likely, or was he the victim of someone else's application of conditioning him (*e.g.*, father Fred Trump or adviser Roy Cohn)? Something to ponder, but since he dismisses most everything that is not his idea would he have realized he was conditioning himself as a victim? This question might be a logical basis for a clinical psychologist's evaluation of the president and perhaps one that has already taken place.[164] A theme for a Netflix® movie ,perhaps? Trump's victim mentality is in large measure based on his refusal to accept criticism. When answering a media question, he uses the oft-repeated aside "you know that better than anybody, but you won't write that" without answering the question and at times more important to him is criticizing a particular reporter. This is usually followed with the comment, "if you take a look at" which is an absolute guarantee of him manipulating information he doesn't understand, prefers to misrepresent or evidence that doesn't exist at all and does not contribute to any sense to the authenticity of his words.

For those who have referred to the dysfunctional 45th presidency as the result of a "Trump virus," it's far worse than that but an appropriate place to start. Just as invasive and horrible as a cancer of the lungs, pancreas, colon, ovaries, bladder, etc., can be, the cancerous Trump presidency has impacted the essence of every citizen, supporters and non-supporters, and many in the global community. Cancer in the body can grow extremely quickly but in less than four years the Trump cancer has occupied and further divided the country and the world at a rapid rate as well. Sooner or later the kimono will be raised, even for viewing by his base of support, and reveal what is underneath. A realistic expectation for Trump to behave with authenticity and transparency has been tossed aside. The best examples of the dismissal of these attributes include uncertainties about the continuing and questionable relationship between the president and Russian President Vladimir Putin, the total bungling of the Covid-19 pandemic with abundant error-filled statements from the president, vice president and numerous staff members, and documented examples of the inner circle of the Trump sphere facilitating the whims and mistakes of Trump the man acting as the president of the US.

The Trump cancer has created its own perception of what authenticity means. Rather than taking action based on a true conformance to facts Trump instead acts on his indomitable personality; it's what I think (believe) so it must be true and therefore it is authentic. Likewise, the Trump understanding of transparency follows a similar approach but, in this case, deceit is his acceptable attribute. It doesn't matter that his pretense is easily recognized rather than acting ethically and morally in a fashion that would communicate a responsible commitment to truth and his oath and to the country. As a result, he thrives on speaking negatively about most things but doesn't assess (care) how this mannerism stifles progress and impairs the construction of unity for the country. Not unlike cancer cells replicating themselves, the Trump cancer prospers on division, building "walls" between loyal and patriotic citizens and between the US and other countries while tearing down morals and alternate opinions that are in his narcissistic way. In one notable moment during an interview Trump took on the energy policy debate and authoritatively stated that if Biden were elected, "no fossil fuels, which means basically no energy…cities would have to be rebuilt because too much lights gets through the windows."[165] Just to be sure he made his point in this interview he also volunteered that there would be no airplanes or cars and made the distinction that under Biden "they don't want to have cows, they don't want to have any form of animals." Yet another moment of clarity.

Cancer doesn't wait for a special moment to inflict harm on the body. Neither does Trump. Both seize every opportunity. In its own way Trump considers himself to be authentic while being transparent only seemingly appears at the least opportune moments. It works in silence until it can no longer hide. It speaks in ways that challenge researchers and medical providers and intimidates its host. It moves around the body at will at its own pace. It resists. It replicates quickly. It just doesn't care what the outcome may be for the individual. In that regard the similarity to the Trump cancer is real as for Trump it is always all about him and the pace of his continually tearing down the country is unrestricted.

"External vigilance is an essential element of a democratic system. A citizenry that takes the good judgment of its leaders for granted is a society that leaves itself vulnerable to disappointment and failure."

———————————— THOMAS JEFFERSON ————————————

The US is indeed vulnerable, disappointed and open to failure on many levels. The Trump cancer has inflicted harm on the country from his first day in office, and possibly even prior to that. When it comes to Trump the country still doesn't know what it doesn't know.

The Trump cancer is far from silent. It is loud, boisterous and untruthful.

The Trump cancer challenges all with its inconsistency, ignorance and narcissism.

The Trump cancer resists all competence, facts and civility.

The Trump cancer has demonstrated that hope for change through its erratic conduct is misplaced hope as it resists at all costs.

The accelerated metastasis of the Trump cancer and its treacherous negative behavior is not hidden as it is front and center in the lives of all Americans.

Trump portrays himself as the victim: the pandemic ruined his economy, the hoax impeachment was intended to torture him , the fake news never gives him credit for anything, the racial protests are Democratic-infused hate crimes against him, and the next election is rigged. And yet, through all the posturing and finger pointing, the cancer was easily identified, and the president was impeached.

The Trump cancer asks why people are not complimenting his genius.

The Trump cancer believes his violent and demeaning rhetoric represents control and power.

The Trump cancer does not have a conscience, but the country does.

The Trump cancer tries to dive deeper into the soul of the country but in light of the protests against the history and presence of systemic race, a different type of resistance is being felt.

The Trump cancer is afraid. Its conflated approach to governing has been discovered on many levels and there are many who feel the country's cure from this disease is not too far away.

There are those who will drink the snake oil delivered by the Trump cancer's brand of sarcasm and lies, if you will, but reality is setting in. Others just shake their heads in disbelief. Unfortunately, truth may come too late for loved ones caught up in the destruction of the pandemic ("the virus is just going to go away"), the treatment suffered by immigrant children and their parents, bigotry and racial slurs voiced toward citizens of color and general chaos fostered by this inept president. He enjoys the chaos. There are many in the administration, the House and the Senate who can make a positive difference by not sitting and waiting for an announcement that the patient, the country, may not make it. It will take a multifaceted effort to overcome the failed promises that began for America and the world on January 20, 2017. It will take time. But working toward clearing out the threats made toward US citizens, removing presidential incompetence and dysfunction and doing so by establishing a basis of truth and trust emanating from a return to authenticity and transparency will provide a formidable prescription to rid the country of the cancerous Trump presidency.

Facts and truth are matters of life and death.
Misinformation, disinformation, delusions and deceit can kill.
Here is what can move us forward:
Science and medicine. Study and knowledge.
Expertise and reason.
In other words, fact and truth.[166]

CHAPTER SEVEN

Accepting This Cancer Is Not an Option

*"Our lives begin to end the day we become silent
about things that matter."*

MARTIN LUTHER KING, JR.

There are medical diagnoses that any individual may be challenged to face during their lives. In these instances, decisions are made with the counsel of medical professionals, at times even with researchers investigating potential new directions in treatment, but certainly with input from family members, clergy and sometimes complemented by information offered by support groups whose members have had to face similar choices. People working together toward a successful outcome for the patient. Ultimately decisions must be made, some with great urgency and others that require a treatment regimen that can last an extended period of time. But when this point in a person's life is reached there will always be the necessity of wrapping hearts and minds around one thing, and that is acceptance. Acceptance of a diagnosis, acceptance of treatment and even acceptance of an outcome.

Acceptance of a diagnosis and acceptance of recommended treatment is most always an anxiety-producing and stressful situation for the patient and all those family members and friends close to the circumstances that have contributed to that moment. Hope for a successful medical outcome for the patient can be influenced by the body of knowledge and experience that researchers and clinicians have provided. The patient and the family in particular tightly grasp hope as it provides some degree of reassurance that their decisions are informed and for the best. Yet, acceptance for some comes with great consequences. A disease that has progressed to a point where when all reasonable steps have been taken can mean acceptance bringing the words "we've done everything we could," or "you need to get your affairs in order," or "come to the hospital right away as he probably won't last through the night." This form of acceptance is difficult and painful. For many it jumpstarts a grieving process, forces thoughts that will require different types of decisions, but nevertheless all equally challenging, complex and demanding. It's an arduous and stressful process.

It's no different for saving the US democracy. The US is at that point right now. The Trump cancer has made lying its most distinctive symptom, but not what would be expected as normal for a president. But there is nothing normal about this president. Even in the face of the coronavirus pandemic Trump exhibited traits most often seen in children: pouting, temper tantrums, taunting those who don't bow to his whims and looking for weaknesses at every turn that he can exploit to his benefit, but not for the benefit of the country. The Trump need for "wins" is somewhat based on his need for control. Controlling a situation is a win for him whether there are substantive results or not and even if the country and citizens lose in the process. Like most things that start and end with him, it's not acceptable for the country.

Four additional years in the White House would allow the Trump cancer to continue to grow. Allow is an important word to focus on when considering a future under Trump. If Republicans retain control of the Senate, they can react in one of two ways. First, they will continue to allow and do Trump's bidding. Many will have ridden Trump's coattails hoping for their own reelection, as well as some representatives in the House, and they will continue to maintain their paranoiac fear of the potential influence Trump might have on their futures if their support is unwavering. Thus the status quo of stonewalling in the Senate will continue and their participation in partisan politics to the detriment of the country will remain intact. Or second, they could recognize that as president for four more years Trump will continue his bizarre ways as president and their best move would be to resist the control that Trump perceives he has over them, and instead Republicans in Congress will actually begin working for the country that they are supposed to be representing. But, either of these scenarios make a gross, and quite literally, an assumption that enough Americans will think that continuing acceptance of the Trump cancer is preferable to any alternative.

Is acceptance of more of the Trump cancer chaos that approaches a totalitarian if not fascist state really the answer the US needs to reclaim its position and respect around the world? Is that acceptance going to unify the country? Is acceptance a means to ending the division the Trump cancer has precipitated and encourages each day? Is acceptance likely to end the Trump cancer racist agenda? Will acceptance remove the Trump cancer authoritarian beliefs routinely exhibited from the Oval Office? Will acceptance provide an incentive for the Trump cancer's most ardent supporters to burrow below the surface of the rhetoric to form a true understanding of the depth of the negative effect this president has on their lives? Trump craves acceptance but acts in ways that do not encourage that outcome for anyone who seeks truth. At a press briefing[167] where he was again defiantly touting hydroxychloroquine as a treatment for Covid-19 in spite of all medical evidence to the contrary, he was asked about the relationship between himself and Dr. Fauci and why the doctor seems to be more popular than him when it comes to receiving trusted information about the coronavirus. His response, "But nobody likes me. It can only be my personality, that's all."[168] Well, that is one important starting point. Perhaps he is striving for the famous Sally

Field moment at the 1985 Oscar ceremony when in her winning acceptance speech she declared, "you like me right now, you like me."[169]

Acceptance of the Trump cancer and everything it represents is unmistakably not the answer. Two very good questions to ask oneself begin with the word why. Why would the country be better off to accept the Trump cancer for another four years? Why would I want support him and vote for him? Draw two columns on a sheet of paper with one labeled pro and the other con. Ignore your sources of information. List the things in each column that you believe to be true. Be honest with yourself, not from a blue or red perspective. Taking the time to try to answer these questions for yourself, not for anyone else, requires throwing out one-word responses, Party affiliation or criticism of the opposing Party or presumptive candidate in 2020. Dig deeper into these things. Don't allow yourself to focus only on the present but instead look to the future. Are there things you believe will get accomplished under Trump that will not be detrimental in a larger sense, at home and abroad? It is not about what he says he is going to do, but rather it is what you believe he is or is not able to accomplish given the divided environment in which we are living that he has created. This exercise is about what you know, not what you are being told. This is about the depth you have personally sought to understand issues that do not reflect rhetoric. There is no right or wrong as you compile your personal pros and cons but the one criterion to follow is truth. Think about Trump's ability to govern and ignore the threats. And, given the history of his first term will he be any more believable or trustworthy?

The Trump cancer is forcing Americans to make an election decision that will have an immediate, and perhaps even more concerning, a lasting impact on the country. If the president is reelected there is every reason to believe that Trump will continue to bring the country down morally as he continues his assault on civility, ethics and trampling on the optimism of Americans. Curiously, as the Covid-19 pandemic continues to grow as a problem not soon to "disappear," there are rifts developing between the GOP and the White

House on several fronts, including Trump's threats about withholding funding from the CDC, a proposed plan to no longer subsidize Covid -19 testing, and proposing to withhold funds from schools closed if they do not reopen. What may be the most insidious view of the Trump mind and lack of understanding or even consideration of what systemic racism is about, is his threat to veto a multifaceted House military spending bill that includes language that has been directed by the Pentagon about the renaming of military bases with Confederacy-era names. Trump opposes this action as it would potentially alienate a large segment of his supporters in the South. This is just another hammer down threat from the child throwing a tantrum. Hence the threat to veto a bill addressing racism and includes the renaming of bases is a true "throwing the baby out with the bath water" approach in classic Trump style. Acceptable logic from the commander in chief? The Senate is on a parallel track with its own legislation and if passed, would require the House and Senate bills to be merged into a single bill. This would present a scenario that if the president did indeed veto the bill, it could create the first potential Congressional override of a veto in his presidency.

It has been shown over and over that the Trump cancer can have a laser focus but mostly only on things he believes are important to him and that he perceives make him more acceptable in his reelection bid. It might be a word, a statistic, a critical comment directed toward him and in one remarkable example his characterization of a test (MoCa)[170] he was given that measures cognitive ability, not intelligence. Although administered earlier in his presidency he brought up the test again and positioned his performance as, "I aced it." With this schoolboy proclamation he must believe his characterization of the test outcome will be more influential and is a tactic he felt would remove all concern about his mental ability. But the truth is this test is only a tool clinicians use to assist in making a differential diagnosis when there are concerns about Parkinson's disease, Alzheimer's, schizophrenia or ALS (Lou Gehrig's Disease). What the MoCa tool is not is an IQ test. It does not provide an assessment of a person's personality, their judgment, decision-making, or their mental acuity at the point in time the test is administered. Results from this test do not provide any guarantee of surfacing early signs of dementia. It is simply a benchmark established for the patient at the point it is administered that might be used later as a point for comparison.

Trump was given this test in 2018 as part of an annual physical exam by then White House physician Ronny Jackson, MD, at the president's request. Was he experiencing symptoms he couldn't explain to himself? Did someone close to him suggest the test would be a good political move? Did he want to prove something to others? In 2018 Trump touted his perfect score of 30 out of 30 questions correct. But take a look at what he said more recently (July 2020).

During an interview on Fox News[171] Trump stated he asked for the test on his last visit to Walter Reed *"a little less than a year ago."* Two problems here: he overlooks the unscheduled trip to Walter Reed in November 2019 and a convenient memory loss for whatever reason, but at any rate the date of the administration of the MoCa test was much further back in time.

He described the test as consisting of *"30 or 35 questions. The first questions are very easy. The last questions are much more difficult, like a memory question."*

Yes, there are questions in eight distinctive areas with different point values assigned for a potential total score of 30. The "difficulty" of the last few questions cover orientation about such things as the date, month, year, day, place and city.

A memory section requires the patient to repeat a set of five words read to the individual. This is done twice. No points are awarded for this exercise, but recall is tested later. *"If you get it in order, you get extra points."*

This is not correct.

"If you -- OK, now he's asking you other questions, other questions. And then 10 minutes, 15, 20 minutes later, they say, remember the first question, not the first, but the 10th question? "If you get it in order, you get extra points."

Later in the test the patient is asked to recall as many of the previous words with no cues given. Recall points are awarded from

0-5 depending on the number of words recalled correctly, but no requirement for recalling them in a certain order, and there are no "extra" points given as this is a distinct question on the test.

Trump in this interview is trying very hard to establish his intelligence but sadly he does not even understand or recount the test correctly. The comments Trump provided in this more recent interview did not speak well for his long-term memory or recall. He will embellish anything, the rare truth or not, if in his mind it makes him seem better, smarter, *i.e.*, acceptable. In this case his description of the MoCa test and his performance are way over the top. So, what's the point? Resurrecting this bit of Trump medical history two years later is mystifying but not out of character for the way the Trump mind engages at any one moment. Is this a ploy to convince his base that he's mentally stable and capable in spite of the disturbing history of his decisions, and threats? Does he think by bringing up this test again it will make him more acceptable in the eyes of Americans in general as the 2020 election approaches? Or is he simply trying to convince himself that he can hang on and is just reinforcing his ego? The MoCa test results, including recognition of a few animals, hardly make his multiplicity of other disquieting symptoms and behaviors go away.

"A man cannot be comfortable without his own approval."

—— MARK TWAIN ——

Polls conducted by a variety of sources routinely cited in the media and touted by campaign staff workers display a variety of data such as the balance of power between political candidates running for office, their positions on issues impacting the country, and more recently voter opinions regarding multiple crises management. Voter satisfaction with the Trump cancer's involvement in crisis management is a difficult poll to conduct. Often the difficulty is having enough specificity in the questions to clearly delineate which crisis is the topic of the poll.

The crisis topics are numerous, of course, as the Trump cancer has become adept at its own participation, from actually creating a crisis to mismanagement of another because of his illogical narcissistic priorities that supersede what was actually required. An article appearing in *The Guardian* titled "The Gap Between Trump's World and Reality is Widening: It's Disturbing to Watch"[172] describes Trump and uses a comparison to Cerebus, a dog monster from Greek mythology with many heads. "One of the creature's heads is obviously Donald Trump's, but there are others, snarling and yapping and bickering, all offering wrong opinions and bad advice as they try to keep Trump in line and do damage control when he strikes out on his own."

A fair description and kudos to the analogy, but the bottom line is that the Trump cancer listens to no one unless he is being told he is right. That is a summation of his character, but it seems many supporters are unconcerned about his character and that is indeed a sad commentary about the US. And yes, it is disturbing to watch. The real travesty is that Trump has the expectation that the country should just accept his opinions, words and priorities and by no means ever, ever question what he does or doesn't' do to improve any crisis situation. Results of a survey published in June 2020 intended to measure opinions about the quality of pandemic information showed "64% of U.S. adults say CDC mostly gets the facts about the outbreak right; only 30% say the same about Trump and his administration."[173] The trend on the part of Americans is a widening degree of distrust in the administration and certainly not blindly accepting statements made by the Trump cancer and those around him. The pandemic is notable as it quickly evolved to a level that Trump early on said would never occur. Even as week by week and month by month Trump understated reality with false claims, made up "facts" and showcased his intelligence by consistently disagreeing with the scientists on his own Task Force.

The situation became worse and just like the magic Trump said would occur in terms of the coronavirus disappearing, he put the devastating pandemic behind him and moved on to doing anything he could think of to bolster his reelection campaign. Positive cases were growing, and people were dying but to an apparent lower level of importance to him than his potential second term. It is hard to imagine that the Trump cancer cares so little about people dying but the evidence is that he prefers instead to bring everything back to him; his intelligence, his television ratings, believe him not anyone else, refuting medical science because he knows better, etc. He even went so far to again promote the use of a drug showing no promise and in fact that had potentially dangerous side effects he showed his lack of knowledge and empathy by offering, "what have you got to lose." As weeks and months passed Trump employed a condescending inflection of his voice when saying the word China. This behavior is so unbelievably childish and habitually occurs when he makes reference to the "China virus," as if that in some way this makes his position stronger and more acceptable to shift focus away from his mismanagement of the pandemic. This tactic began in the earliest days of the pandemic and continues. The Trump cancer once again overlooks an extremely important point. It's not the China virus, it is now very much the Trump virus. Own it Mr. President, in the US it's yours.

Next crisis, the economy. The pandemic hit Trump where it hurt. The one and only positive thing he had to talk about going into his bid for reelection that might have universal appeal among voters was the economy. He and his cronies horribly underestimated the toll the pandemic would take on every American and the "only I can fix it" president fixed nothing. In fact, the absence of early and what would have been appropriate steps that could and should have been taken in combating the pandemic were relegated to obscurity in favor of an out of control ego and political manipulations. Small businesses were crushed while bailouts went to corporations and industries that would see their business suffer. Airlines, for example, may have received funds but people were still not flying for fear of contracting the coronavirus at airports, on planes, in rental cars, etc., and over time the help given airlines would prove to be insufficient. Unemployment figures escalated each week, yet the Trump cancer wanted to talk about how many jobs were benefiting blacks, but this too was typical slight of hand data maneuvering and did not address jobs lost that were destined not to return for those individuals and looking only at employment numbers gave false hope. By "forcing" his Republican governors to reopen from their lockdown state, encouraging all businesses to reopen and all Americans to get back to work, the Trump cancer was exploiting its own need with a lack of insight, understanding and lack of acceptance of coronavirus data on many levels. Many businesses that had been shuttered were no longer viable to reopen.

As some states began to reopen and others adopted a more cautious approach, the "it will disappear" president faced a resurgence of Covid-19 cases diagnosed and the number of deaths grew as well. Over a period of months, the surges became more prevalent and lasting and some states were forced to roll back their first reopening steps. States most impacted by the surge of coronavirus growth included several that were key in Trump's reelection bid. The economy? In general, the Trump emphasis on reopening to stimulate economic recovery did not fare well, not at all in some segments, and the filing of escalating unemployment claims continued week after week. Some economic experts found themselves not only concerned about the present recession and also feared it would ramp up to a full-fledged depression. Trump does not make a distinction between the economy and the stock market. He prefers to focus on the stock market as a sign of the recovery and how well that serves Americans. He conveniently forgets that only 55 percent of Americans own a stock and that figure includes those who participate in mutual funds through their 401k retirement programs.[174] This is not an attractive fact or acceptable reality for the promise-them-everything-with-no-facts-president. What the Trump cancer never understood were that the models used to predict the impact of the coronavirus are based on many proven analytical factors. If businesses did not cooperate by closing their doors the vast number of deaths would have been exponentially higher, but in Trump's mind the human cost was of a lesser importance.

A level of economic recovery would eventually occur, but not in a rapid fashion, and potentially reveal opportunities not apparent prior to the pandemic but lives lost are lives lost forever. Yes, it is an unattractive trade, a damaged economy vs. death. The cyclical suppression of the infection curve through individual mitigation behaviors and business restrictions, followed by the too soon reopening of businesses encouraged/demanded by Trump, a resurgence of infections rising again and businesses closing again is not a solution. An assessment of the benefit to the economy vs. the risk of more American lives lost following this potentially repetitive scenario unfortunately does not present a defensible picture to those only parochially oriented to dollars and cents. Adding the up and down occurrences of the coronavirus with the reopening of schools at all educational levels along with necessary mitigation plans, also requires recognition that problems will multiply for children, their families, teachers, and staff on both the economic and health fronts. Trump's simplistic desire to reopen schools is not based on a sound assessment of the multitude of issues that must be addressed. He only wants to check a box.

Repeatedly the Trump cancer put the pandemic behind him, and to a lesser degree the economy, as he had moved his most profound attention to the reelection crisis surfacing before his eyes as he spewed forth an increased level of unsubstantiated claims and manipulation of information to make it support his reelection campaign. But then came unrest around the country. There is no question that the Trump cancer was an instigator of sorts in the next crisis he faced in the form of the BLM protests that continued to grow week after week. He did not provide demonstrable presidential attention and actions but instead made threats and engaged in conflicts with mayors and governors attempting to manage the problems in their locales. Two days after his 2017 inauguration Trump stated, "Peaceful protests are a hallmark of our democracy. Even if I don't agree, I recognize the rights of people to express their views."[175] As the protests continued his impatience with the ineffectiveness of his half-hearted attempts to calm the country, he began to play in his conspiracy world, *i.e.*, name calling and ultimatums delivered most frequently through his tweets. He totally lost sight of what the protests were about but instead focused on what appeared to be an invasion of individuals creating havoc in cities where peaceful protests were occurring and lumped them all together. In a statement delivered in his stilted style while leaning on the lectern just prior to the now infamous Bible photo opp he proclaimed, "I am your President of law and order." On this occasion his remarks ranged in content from protecting Second Amendment rights, instructing mayors and governors to establish a law enforcement presence and sending in the US military if this was not done, to steps being taken in DC in particular accompanied by his threats and penalties for protestors. At some point in his tenure president Trump had heard the phrase, rule of law, that now he and his enablers attempt to use to their advantage in spite of the Trump cancer's consistent thumbing of his nose to the concept. Below is Trump's interpretation of what rule of law means.

"One law and order — and that is what it is: one law. We have one beautiful law. And once that is restored and fully restored, we will help you, we will help your business, and we will help your family. America is founded upon the rule of law."[176]

Is this twisted misrepresentation revealing his true feelings acceptable from a president who has consistently attempted to avoid the rule of law and bastardizes its very existence with his resistance to it as a tenet of our democracy? As the protests continued his statements became more authoritarian and continued to show racial overtones that were both invasive and incendiary at the same time. The original intent of the protests to bring focus to police brutality focused on black and brown communities across the country became lost. What began as peaceful assemblies sparked by the Floyd murder became infiltrated by angry elements resorting to violence that served no purpose other than generating negativism towards all. It is unfortunate that the actions of violence, looting and encroachment on aspects of authority occurred when more significant progress could have been made. The threats, and reality, of sending in non-requested and non-identified policing forces to cities such as Portland, OR and Chicago, IL, and use of highly criticized enforcement tactics on citizens was irreparably tied to the Trump cancer reboot of portraying himself as the law and order president. Previously he had self-proclaimed his identity as the "wartime" president when facing the pandemic. And how did these identity transformations work for the president? Again, not well at all as the president appeared as child constantly changing what he wants to be when he grows up; today a cowboy, tomorrow a fireman and the next day a professional athlete. Trump hasn't reached the grown-up stage, so more wanna-be portrayals are undoubtedly on the horizon.

It took only a week for the Trump cancer to retreat from the attempted pivot to an image of a concerned and empathetic president, that was so out of character given the entire history of Trump as president. It was back to familiar chaotic territory of false claims about the pandemic, promoting an ineffective drug, pushing states and schools to reopen, criticizing protests instead of formulating a plan to address issues, and most anything else that crossed his mind. It was an implosion under fire of massive proportions from the realities of multiple crises, his sinking approval rating and his ratings in pre-election polls against the presumptive Democratic candidate going south at a rapid pace, particularly in key battleground states around the country.

There is little respect for Trump around the world fostered by his past actions, and now disappointment from his slipshod pandemic response, his ridicule of other world leaders and his wonderful friendship for Vladimir Putin and love for Kim Jong Un. His relationship with President Xi Jinping is on the rocks. He has shifted from the "greatest deal ever made" with China to now saying "I may never speak to him again." He professes great friendships when he feels it serves him in an advantageous way, but he is also dependably quick to tear down those "friendships" and criticize when things don't go his way, or he seeks an out to deflect blame that is or may be directed at him. The exception throughout his presidency is of course the mysterious, concerning relationship with Putin. The mystery will eventually be solved but not from anything revealed by Trump, unless by accident. The bipartisan Senate Select Committee on Intelligence has put its findings on the table from an in-depth assessment, not limited to criminal misconduct, that shows Russian interference in the 2016 election, how it was done and ways in which the Trump campaign was accepting help.[177] The report also contradicts Trump's written testimony to Robert Mueller that he did not discuss the Russian hacked Wikileaks emails with Roger Stone, a convicted and now pardoned friend of Trump. Senate Republicans, Trump family members and others continue to bang the no collusion drum, but it would appear that the drumhead is splitting before their eyes.

The areas of control that Trump fails at routinely are his disturbing verbal comments and his texting. He is a "loose cannon" rolling around the country's deck. It is quite impossible to categorize his behavior as accidental. Rather the content that is spontaneous, offensive, uncontrolled, manipulative and false, and on many occasions creates fear and incites violence. It is just who he is, and the public will be subject to his mental inadequacy as long as he has a speaking forum or technological platform of any kind. At this stage of his presidency, or ever for that matter, there is no reasonable expectation that the Trump cancer will change to make the man or his actions acceptable. All Americans have, or want, to respect the office of the president but Trump does nothing to encourage that behavior or as former Secretary of State Margaret Albright stated early in 2018, "the chair of the leader of the free world is empty."[178] Two years later the chair remains empty but is now adorned with the failures that makes it quite impossible for that leadership chair to ever be occupied by Trump. There are those who will follow him off the cliff and deny to the end that all claims against Trump are false. It is his personal pandemic. Just like the larger pandemic impacting all Americans in 2020 and beyond Trump has no cure for his personal pandemic. He doesn't have a cure because he doesn't recognize or accept that he is ill, and that his disease has spread rapidly across the country and the world. There is no balance. He's insecure. He is impulsive. His knowledge on most subjects is sorely lacking. His appreciation for most anything that does not provide him with profit in some way is unimportant. This is not a deserving president of the US. His personal cancerous ways have enveloped him. This is a person who needs to get out of the way of the country. He needs to return to his narcissistic and obsessive behaviors, his perversions, counting his gold in private, and in no way have any influence on the future of Americans or the country.

"Failure is simply the opportunity to begin again, this time more intelligently."

— HENRY FORD —

The Trump presidency whenever it may end will not be judged favorably and, in many respects, will be only viewed as a failed attempt for personal greatness to achieve his status as a martyr. The country will need to begin again and seek to move beyond partisan choices and instead evaluate the character of the person to be at the helm and the qualities that contribute to that individual's ability to lead.

EPILOGUE

Cancer can invade anyone's body, anytime and at any age. Cancer doesn't wait for discovery to start its incursion into the body. It can stay silent and undetected until it is revealed serendipitously or through a search incorporating considerable testing and so that a differential diagnosis can be made. For many the diagnosis may leave little hope for recovery and a cascade of events begins, including an introspective assessment of one's life and those who have played important roles in it along the way, conversations with family and friends, and preparing oneself as best as possible for what may come. Treatments of one form or another may be undertaken and frequently a combination of chemotherapy, radiation and even surgery may produce a remission and prolong a life, but a favorable outcome may only be measured in weeks, survival for a small number of years and for some a longer-term remission.

Yes, there are miraculous instances when against all odds an individual's acceptance of a previous personal terminal consequence was suddenly and remarkably incorrect. In these situations the patient, and all those close to the reality of their combined hopelessness, find that the ticking clock predicting a potential time for an imminent death has been replaced by a refreshing new outlook for life, an appreciation for what can be left behind and replaced by a focus on what lies ahead; a true celebration of life.

With all of the positive patient outcomes that occur thanks to ever-expanding medical knowledge and innovative treatment regimens one fact remains startlingly clear. Cancer undetected, untreated, unresponsive or resistant, will kill the patient. For the benefit of the US and its citizens facing the negativity of the Trump cancerous presidency, vigilance is required for the survival of the democracy, rule of law, civility and recognition of the country's needs and the actions required to effectively fulfill them.

"We are taught you must blame your father, your sisters, your brothers, the school, the teachers – but never blame yourself. It's never your fault. But it's always your fault, because if you wanted to change you're the one who has got to change."

—————— KATHERINE HEPBURN ——————

The Trump cancer witnessed each day is a work in progress because what is consistently exposed is only change for the worse. Trump sees no advantage in changing anything about himself, only taking advantage of others. There can be no expectation that this narcissistic, xenophobic, misogynistic and unbalanced individual thrust into the lives of Americans and cultures around the world can change. He has no motivation to change as the routine is to direct blame toward others for whatever and however he may be accused of being the precipitating cause of damage and general failure. He won't change in any way because he will never want to change. It must be a curse to feel one is so perfect in every way that it is the responsibility of others to just get in line and assume that they must recognize that any change required is for them to undertake.

As citizens, the ongoing after-effects of the cancerous Trump presidency will have impacted literally everyone in one way or another, from children to senior citizens because the trail of this multifaceted cancer is so bizarre on so many levels. It is also disconcerting that acceptance of his many uninformed raids on the country by some is, well, acceptable. When someone learns about a cancer diagnosis there is a tendency to go through common stages of emotional wrangling (denial, anger, bargaining, sadness and depression), and finally to acceptance. But ultimately each person's journey is different. Experiencing cancer is a very personal thing but there are resources to help people through the process. In the case of the Trump cancer, deniability of responsibility and accountability has become the go-to performance standard for Trump himself. The Trump cancer has experienced resistance from the country as Americans determine to not let the scourge continue and damage the fabric of the country using the interventions at their disposal.

The country will be resilient, it has been since its very beginnings, and will work hard to survive the lies, racism, xenophobic fears, bias, bigotry, narcissism, endless misrepresentations and claims. Even the Trump ideology, his "I Party," that has usurped the Republican party and abandoned its historic conservative principles must be shelved. If Trump were to be reelected, it will precipitate a time of fear. What will he do next? Without the boundaries set by constant fundraising events to pay for a presidential campaign, without the pressure of time and commitments of running for office will result with essentially no fences around him at all to prevent him from continuing his assault on the country and the world. There are many who look at that potential future prospect as the end of the US democracy. The country will not have guard rails to protect itself from even further uncontrolled cancerous confrontations. Perhaps that is a bit strong, but what is certain is that he will take full advantage of any and all opportunities to work for personal gain in whatever forms that might take.

As his niece, a clinical psychologist, alleged in her timely book, what is seen today in the way Trump behaves mirrors the behaviors she had witnessed in his youth.[145] It seems from her analysis that the Trump cancer will go further to make its next four years even more chaotic. Think about that. The Trump cancer during the first term markedly divided the country in many ways, including a decided bipartisan divide in accomplishing legislative successes. He demonstrated his ability to incite violence and racial unrest. He showed a lack of any empathy when speaking, particularly about the pandemic and its toll on the health of Americans. He continued his "I know everything" mentality and in effect reinforced every negative characteristic that has reached heighted levels "never seen before." His need, yes need, to be right, regardless of facts to the contrary, suggests that his lust for martyrdom drives every comment. Every interaction with those whose knowledge far exceeds his own, every interaction with allies, every interaction with the US and foreign media, every demand and threat made regardless of the target audience and absent of any lucid basis he will raise the bar to a higher level of chaos while simultaneously lowering it to achieve personal gain. He assumes, demands if he could, that none of these examples and many others are not to be questioned or criticized.

If the Trump cancer continues to ignore the rule of law, create division between the branches of government, attempt to overreach the authority of the executive branch and ignore the separation of powers, the country will suffer immensely. There is already significant recovery to be addressed once the cancer is excised. The end of Trump's attempt at autocratic reign and quest for martyrdom will not soon be resolved because of the damage he has created thus far. Time will be needed for the country to heal, for important international relationships to be renewed and time will also surely reveal the extent of the disease that he and his administration lemmings have cultivated and hidden. Trump's personal abuse of power driven by a lack of skill, governing knowledge and abject incompetence has been supported by the majority leader in the Senate and Republicans in the Senate and the House and those leading states as governors. They will find that their fear of Trump's influence on their job security and their reelection has been misplaced. They too were not spared the cancer propagated by Trump as the metastasis of his boorish cancerous conduct is on their record now, and explanations will be sought when a post-mortem assessment is convened the next time they are on a ballot. Will they be given a pass? Will they be held accountable for representing Trump instead of their actual voters? "Don't look back. Something may be gaining on you."[179]

The Trump cancer's approach to the office of the presidency has been quite simple because as complex as he may have appeared, he is decidedly a simple man-child. He rarely thought before he spoke, and it was as if he was pouting because he did not receive his requested McDonald's Happy Meal® and its enclosed plastic toy. What he was able to speak was rarely clear, with the exception of insults and derogatory names he attached to anyone he chose to criticize. He may have thought name calling was cute or just that his base would appreciate them, but in actuality they make him seem more pathetic and childlike and hardly representative of a president of the US. His personal toolbox contained only two items, lies and false claims which he used with great frequency and with the most significant outcome being media reporting to which he responded by using these same tools again and again.

Sun Tzu's "all warfare is based on deception" is unquestionably part of the Trump cancer's playbook. Cancer in the body is deceptive as well. It may appear to be weakening at some point only later to reveal its continuing strength through the destruction of cells elsewhere in the body. The Trump cancer has accomplished a similar detrimental effect through distractions, shiny objects as some have termed them, to draw focus away from what in actuality may be his misguided agenda and his own "deceptive art."

It is better to offer no excuse than a bad one.
—————— GEORGE WASHINGTON ——————

Trump has fooled and deceived many people, from the primaries to his election and during the nearly four years since his inauguration. However, he has not fooled anyone who thinks they do not need his endorsement or to some degree are not concerned of staying out of his crosshairs, misaligned and out of synch as they may be. World leaders, for example, see through everything that is Trump as he and family members have been openly mocked. Qualified leaders of other countries recognized quickly that Trump cannot carry out a conversation or negotiation based on facts. They have learned that he does not consider or understand the near and long-term ramifications of what he believes are bold and decisive moves. They only represent things to just put up on the Trump "scoreboard" regardless of their consequences to the US and others. The watchdog media recognized his deceptive behavior from the outset, frankly even before he entered the political arena as a presidential candidate. When the errors, false claims and lies are exposed by the media, and other individuals as well for that matter, they receive the patented Trump response of a pointed attack. These attacks nearly always consist of unrelated derogatory and demeaning criticisms whether they are delivered verbally or in tweets. It is his routine to place blame on most every topic anywhere—Democrats, the media, China, past presidents, members of NATO—but certainly not upon himself. Like cancer can be at times, and with Trump at all times, Trump and cancer are brothers in their approach to the world, predictably unpredictable in knowing where harm will be created next.

The real catastrophe of Trump's reality show in which he stars as acting president is that there is no script and no real strategy or plan. The best example of this is clearly exhibited by the rollercoaster bungling of the coronavirus pandemic. Each daily episode was as disjointed as the previous one but with a common scheme of leaving adequate room to promote himself. It is the Trump form of cancer that riddles his mind. He just doesn't care what anyone else thinks with the exception of those he wants most to manipulate be they a foreign leader or those Americans from whom he seeks their votes. As he has nurtured his cancer tactics, he has consistently chosen what he believes to be vulnerable targets toward which he can direct his form of destructive insurgency, and habitually in his administration he removes those who won't or don't bend to his will. Another way to think about his attacks is that his "style" is more like guerilla warfare tactics. There are no front lines in his personal war on the country. Whatever crosses the Trump blood brain barrier is the next target. At times it doesn't seem that there is even a clear objective but rather just an attack as a means to show his perceived superiority and authority.

Cancer in the body doesn't care who it poisons, the havoc it wreaks on those suffering, their families, the healthcare system, productivity for individuals in the workplace or its impact on the economy. Neither do any of these things categorically bother Trump with the exception of, perhaps, the economy or at least his focus on personal gain, but even on this topic there are unknowns regarding his true personal motives. For the rest of us there is a need to remove his exaggerations because the facts he uses resemble swiss cheese at a delicatessen. He is all about thinking, feeling and stating that he won something. He evokes scenarios like racial hatred, back-handed complements directed toward white supremacists and at every turn employing fear mongering in a contemptable attempt to garner votes. He has poisoned American society, its institutions and for many their way of life, all while presenting himself as the guru of all things as the "stable genius." From the beginning of his presidency he billed himself as the best ever president, with no real understanding of the accomplishments of prior presidents of his Party much less governing. He assumes that a positive legacy of his time in office is assured. He will indeed be remembered but more likely as a case study of how not to be leader or a great president.

In spite of his frequently stated opinion, he is the antithesis of a genius. It is the collective will of the people that provide stability and it is their experiences, expertise and common sense that truly guide the country. Americans are the family and caregivers of our country, and as our democracy dictates, the control and cure for the disease that now has metastasized and looms over our lives with the Trump presidency is in our hands. Because he didn't know that Abraham Lincoln was a Republican, he most likely also didn't know about Lincoln's commitment to truth.

"I am a firm believer in the people. If given the truth, they can be depended upon to meet any national crisis. The great point is to bring them the real facts."

———————— ABRAHAM LINCOLN ————————

In general, seeking a nirvana environment at a time when the country's institutions are functioning at full efficiency and when all Americans will endorse and enjoy every characteristic and action by its president, would rarely if ever occur. But with this president, the invasion of the Trump cancer has shown that incoherent incompetence resides in the Oval Office. On a daily basis, OMG moments are revealed that are shocking; he did or said what? It is easy to throw up one's hands at times in reaction to this president because he is so out of place, but there is nothing humorous about the bedlam he has created. The Trump presidency characterized by narcissistic leanings that are supported by others has and continues, at this writing, to provide little real comfort or confidence for what lay ahead.

The Trump cancer ineptitude is growing every day and the Covid-19 pandemic illustrates clearly that leadership, truth and proficiency are factors missing from Trump's ability. The public must consistently and continuously ask the question, "when will we become more important than partisan politics and individual agendas when our lives are quite literally at stake on such a large scale?" Isn't the health and education of the country's children more important than paying more attention to his win column? "We're all in this together" is the often heard and true statement regarding the pandemic. This is a strong position that the country has demonstrated repeatedly. But the difference now is that the country is not being led. The hope is for a resolution everyone wishes would come sooner, not later. Americans pray for as minimal a devastating outcome as possible. It is unmistakable that the needed leadership to bring the country through this crisis will come from the masses, not this president. The Trump cancer has moved on from the pandemic and instead focuses on personal priorities that he believes will be more beneficial for him. Those around him are facilitators and push their own agendas while they imply that they support his. What has happened to America?

The Trump cancer is looking for an individual win, by his definition, over anything. The pandemic health crisis. Restoring the economy. Racism, but only by his perceptions of what those wins may look like. Education for children. Civility, compassion and empathy…sorry, wrong guy. But the Trump cancer shows that he has no ability much less a plan to do these positive things as he desperately tries to convince the country to give him another term to continue to inflict mayhem, turmoil and devastation on the morals of the country. In a growing number of ways possible wins are going away for the Trump. He is following a growing list of losing paths. It's past time for Trump to be set aside while his quest for someone calling him a hero has long since passed. Using a favorite Trump descriptor, however, calling him a loser is gaining momentum.

The inability of Trump to put his id aside is taking the country to ruin. It is not simply a matter of campaign promises not being met. Rather, the daily onslaught of the Trump-centric demonstrations of his lack of understanding and applicable knowledge increase as he becomes more desperate and his tweets become more bizarre. His attempts at presenting himself as caring and empathetic and sober to the health crisis facing the US and the world is absent. It is hard to ignore the many ways in which the Trump cancer has provided aid and comfort to the pandemic enemy.

Most concerning to this writer is that Trump has divided the country in ways that may have been fearfully thought about during the Republican Party primary debates in 2015 but reason dictated that they would surely not occur if he were elected. At the time just thinking about the possibility was disturbing in that there would have had to be others that applauded his every word, even if they knew that by doing so they were being complicit to the potential detrimental impact Trump may have on the country. But what has materialized is beyond what may have been feared or even imagined. To say that the Trump cancer doesn't care beyond the boundaries of his minimal abilities while putting himself first above all just doesn't go far enough. The Trump cancer makes a habit of using his finely-honed skill of exaggeration and embellishment of false facts just to reinforce any controversy that he seems to thrive on. Ethics? Moral values? Truth-teller?

This is the United States. And because the country is based on democratic principles its citizens have never been nor have to be in one-hundred percent agreement about anything. That is as it should be. Each person has the freedom to express opinion and support for who and what is important to them, including the president of the moment, but being so committed to a man and an ideology does not pull down the mask that is disguising intent, motive or personal outcomes. To be so resistant to the detrimental evidence that mounts each day is actually doing oneself a disservice. There will be a time when each person will assess the right or wrong of their position on the 45th president and his version of authenticity. In the meantime, each person has the sanctity of his/her own mind, their observations, and their one vote. Together those votes may become a targeted therapy to eradicate the Trump cancer from a continuation of the ongoing devastation on the country and the stain it has placed on the Constitution, the people and the reputation of the US around the world. A complete remission from the damage to the cellular makeup of our institutions, the quite literal health of our nation and our very futures will be a long and painful struggle. But this nation can come together. It's been done before though the recovery this time will be the result of focusing on more than one internal pandemic fostered by the president. Resilience is the word most often used in historical commentaries about the past to describe the country's forthright and moral destiny to a rebirth. Heads up, hearts beating, our chests out and renewal of patriotic faith and commitment…we can do this.

The Democratic Party election ticket for 2020 is a significant contrast to what the country has experienced from the Trump/Pence duo. Should the Vice President Joe Biden and Senator Kamala Harris nominees win the election, the recovery cycle that will need to begin to overcome what Trump has left behind will be significant. Trump assuredly will make considerable noise if he loses, but the new administration will likely do its best to focus forward. Unlike Trump who chooses to look the other direction and criticize multiple presidencies that preceded him it is probably safe to assume that the less said about Trump the better, giving little oxygen to mistakes of the past. If Trump is reelected, particularly if he is successful in suppressing voting across the country, Americans can expect more of the uninformed impulsive decisions and rejection of advice that have become the norm, and perhaps some decisions that will have even more significant negative consequences. It is well established that history is a predictor of future occurrences and the Trump presidency has little to boast about that is positive, helpful to the country and world allies or represents meeting the needs of Americans. His tactics would remain the same, but louder with more capital letters in his tweets. In the face of what seems to be string of resistance tactics prepared by Trump's attorneys that the judicial system at different levels have rebuked because of their lack of merit, it could be interesting. Unlike the approach he tried with his prior business lawsuits, federal checks and balances could be his ultimate downfall.

The Trump cancer doesn't care about me. I can live with that. I've had cancer before. He really doesn't care about his supporters. They only represent a means to a personal end. He let Americans down and played to their weaknesses like pawns in a game of chess. He let the country down. He let the world down. Can Trump live serenely out of office knowing the cancer that he and his cronies spread over the country will by necessity foster a necessary, long and painful recovery for Americans? His character traits answer this question easily. Yes, he thinks he will just move on to create his next debacle to salve his insecure ego. He will find ways to create havoc in some form or another to demonstrate how right he was as president, endlessly accuse the country of voter fraud with an election loss if that occurs, but eventually he will pay a price when his inherited presidential protections disappear. Many of the skeletons are already out of the closet and they won't go away. The country's judicial system will continue to seek him out and apply the rule of law. He will not be allowed to "go gently into the dark night,"[180] because the principles, institutions and laws of the US system of order and character, that he sought to make over through his own rough and careless acts and ignorance, will ultimately prevail. Working the system as president for personal benefit is inexcusably wrong. If there is funding to be applied to a traditional presidential library there will be nothing traditional about it if it is built, as most likely it will resemble a carnival side show with barkers barking.

A component of Trump supporters who do not care deeply enough about what has happened to the morality of the country and cannot remove their cloak of partisanship are in effect being complicit to the damage the Trump cancer has inflicted. Trump is so overwhelmingly oriented to liking anyone who likes him that he endorses groups whose goals are decidedly detrimental to the country. In his sleep me must hear, "QAnon likes me, great. KKK likes me, terrific. White supremacists support me, wonderful." He just returns what he thinks are compliments. His ignorance of their motives desired outcomes must remain a mystery to him, but he has no hesitancy about using these factions to his advantage. He will use anyone and anything for a perceived "win." The frequent labels of fake and hoax that Trump applies to challenges or the discovery of his own actions will not change what he has done. Name calling and threats will not have any affect other than contributing to the legacy of his inappropriate rhetoric. Looking for truth cannot authoritatively or responsibly be positioned as inappropriate, but not seeking truth does a disservice for all Americans. Trump has no respect for anyone unless those individuals will benefit him. But respect really isn't the right word. He cares about himself and in that way he becomes his own enemy. With loyalty being such an important part of what he looks for in individuals, he is disloyal to himself through his lack of personal control.

As the country learns more and more about how the Trump cancer has betrayed his oath of office and how in the process, he has so negatively impacted the lives, and deaths, of so many Americans, answering the question of "what's next" is not just an academic exercise. Americans must make a choice. Does truth matter or is manipulation the path down which they wish to be led? The answer is not about making a parochial political choice. Some profess it's about selecting the less of two evils when voting for a presidential candidate. No, Americans must take control of their destiny.

Truth will be the final determinant but waiting for that truth through another Trump term of office or even years later is also not the answer. Americans must take a step back now and ask themselves "is a continuation of irresponsible and incompetent governing what I want for myself, my family and my country?"

The saga continues and perhaps it was inevitable given past behaviors, as it was confirmed that Trump has contracted Covid-19. Throughout the months that the US and the world has had to face the pandemic, Trump refused to acknowledge just how serious a threat to health that the virus was, is, to all…everyone. His informed awareness did not motivate him to personally comply with the steps that science was advocating, yet the White House guidelines and the infamous "15 days to slow the spread" issued in March 2020, had the Trump/Pence thumbprints firmly applied. Later the specific mitigation steps advocated by the White House Task Force and the CDC were also apparently not meant for Trump. He preferred to try to represent himself as the expert, science be damned.

There can be no denial of the extent of Trump's knowledge about the threat for months beginning in January 2020 as Bob Woodward responsibly recorded his conversations with the president as he was working to finalize his latest book, *Rage*. Trump had in effect given his informed consent to the recordings as Woodward continually reminded him that their conversations were being recorded. Throughout the period of the multiple interviews much was occurring in terms of the steps being taken to both prepare for and respond to the growing number of positive cases and deaths in the US. Trump's expertise reality had traveled over a great distance from a point of his insistence that "we have this totally under control" to waking up to the genuineness that he had tested positive for the virus.

The extent to how seriously his health was impaired following acknowledgement of his positive test precipitated what has become the norm for Trump and his administration. Statements, from a variety of administration sources, did little to provide the country with transparency about his condition. It became a matter of covering up the original cover up, *i.e.*, Trump is fine and doing great and the virus will miraculously disappear. The onslaught of contradictory information coming from the White House and his inner circle about Trump's health is beyond frustrating while Trump himself tweets in all caps with accusations about numerous political issues as the 2020 election loomed larger in the foreground, the push to approve a Supreme Court nominee, the dysfunction of the administration in general, questionable activities of the Republican-controlled Senate under the leadership of McConnell, and more.

The medical updates provided and filtered through Trump's White House physician, Sean Conley, DO, were widely questioned by medical professionals around the country. Over several days a flurry of misspeaks and walk backs by Dr. Conley took place to clarify information, but in essence more questions were created that remained unanswered and the data that might provide insight never shared. It seems that if he had had an appendectomy the public would have learned more than what was being shared about Trump's match against Covid-19. When there were updates given on the steps outside of Walter Reed Hospital, behind Trump's physician at the lectern were a team of physicians serving in the role of background singers and props that were never heard. The question why they were not participants in delivering information can only be answered with the suspicion that in some fashion they were gagged to provide truth that was in opposition to Dr. Conley's remarks and answers to media questions.

As further evidence to demonstrate his focus to diminish the severity of his Covid-19 infection and ruminating while in the hospital about him appearing weak, it became untenable for Trump to admit that he was as vulnerable to the virus as anyone else. He apparently insisted that he be driven around the vicinity of Walter Reed Hospital to wave at sidewalk crowds who had gathered to support him. In spite of cautions given, he overruled doctors and the Secret Service and made the joy ride, jeopardizing many who were around him inside the vehicle and in and outside the confines of the hospital. The vehicle in question is hermetically sealed as a security protection for the president in normal circumstances, but on this occasion the Secret Service agents were put in danger. Air circulation is left to what was inside the vehicle. These agents are prepared to die in their role to protect the president, but does this commitment apply to the dangerous behavior of the president himself?

And then came a video message. He stated he had learned much about the virus while undergoing treatment, but it does give one pause to think that for nine months he ignored facts, scientific expertise and he did not transparently share critical knowledge with the public that would have had essential positive effect. But he authoritatively shared in the video, " we will beat the virus as a country," apparently conveniently forgetting how much he personally was responsible for damage to the country and its citizens. The totality of his negative management is yet to be fully understood as the number of cases and deaths continue to increase.

While hospitalized Trump reverted back to his 'I' philosophy and brought the spotlight back to him as he spewed forth with more false claims and absurdities while being imposed upon with a true and personal shelter in place existence. Desperate to somehow support his reelection bid, on October 5 the day he left the hospital, Trump tweeted a variety of his most frequently used campaign promises, most in all caps as his means of shouting.

"SAVE OUR SECOND AMENDMENT. VOTE!"
"FIGHT THE CORRUPT FAKE NEWS MEDIA. VOTE!"
"PROTECT PREEXISTING CONDITIONS. VOTE!"
"BETTER & CHEAPER HEALTHCARE. VOTE!"
"PRO LIFE! VOTE!"
"SPACE FORCE. VOTE!"
"BEST V.A. EVER. 91% APPROVAL RATING. VOTE!"
"401 (K). VOTE!"
"BIGGEST TAX CUT EVER, AND ANOTHER ONE COMING. VOTE!"
"RELIGIOUS LIBERTY. VOTE!"
"LAW & ORDER. VOTE!"
"STRONGEST EVER MILITARY. VOTE!"
"STOCK MARKET HIGHS. VOTE!"

"Virginia Voters! Your Governor wants to obliterate your Second Amendment. I have stopped him. I am the only thing between you and your Second Amendment. Working hard in Virginia. It's IN PLAY. Better Vote for your favorite President, or wave goodbye to low taxes and gun rights!"

Shorthand comments that are meant to incite and not necessarily encourage responsible voting. On the same day consider this tweet from the hospital as he anticipated an early discharge to the White House.

"I will be leaving the great Walter Reed Medical Center today at 6:30 P.M. Feeling really good! Don't be afraid of Covid. Don't let it dominate your life. We have developed, under the Trump Administration, some really great drugs & knowledge. I feel better than I did 20 years ago!"

How can anyone, much less the president of a country with over 200,000 deaths and millions of positive Covid-19 cases on the books, tell Americans to not be afraid of this deadly virus or not to be concerned about its potential effects on their lives and those important to them. Totally irresponsible is not a strong enough rebuke of such statements. Will he feel that way if a family member dies from the virus? Should American's respond with, "Oh well, they weren't afraid."

An early orchestrated discharge allows Trump to return to the inappropriate behaviors that conceivably contributed to many positive Covid-19 cases with members of his inner circle, senators, and at events that may turn out to be super-spreader activities. This move is difficult to review beyond a political maneuver, a staged public relations event and worse, a misrepresentation of the importance of what is taking place in the US that is impacting the entire population. Leaving the hospital and returning to the White House places many individuals in harm's way and in an environment that a lack of proactive contact tracing that has not occurred. in any possible definition of that word as he potentially threatens the health of many.

"We do not lack devices for measuring these miserable days of ours in which it should be our pleasure that they be not frittered away without leaving behind any memory of ourselves in the mind of men."[181]

LEONARDO DA VINCI

There will indeed be memories of the Trump cancer, its negativism and the self-fulfilling prophecy of failure to achieve a position of martyrdom, a position that only he feels he deserves. Instead what Trump has achieved, however, is a place in history as an impeached president, one who placed himself above the country, speaking lies instead of truth, and one who did far more to divide the country rather than uniting it in an era of multiple crises. Americans can handle the truth, but the 45th president cannot recognize it or accept it. His destiny will be reading the final page of the Trump presidency post-mortem and it will simply read, "you're fired."

ACKNOWLEDGEMENTS

To pursue a project such as this requires that it not be undertaken lightly as research dictates direction and content and the task becomes dependent on support from others. To that point I first acknowledge the encouragement from family, friends and academic colleagues to push me forward even during a period of down time when I was recovering from two orthopedic surgeries.

Above all I want to acknowledge a group influence that provided the ultimate motivation to carry my writing to an end. I am speaking about Americans and the country that provides incredible opportunities for us all. Overcoming division is possible because the tools for change rest in our hands. Whatever differences exist in ideological orientation between citizens, it is well to remember that the US was founded on principles, not money. Leadership from the time the country was established is what put American on a path to greatness, not slogans and lies. Healthy, evidence-based debate following its declaration of independence continued to refine the newly launched nation through the Constitution and adherence to the rule of law. Opinions varied along the way. Differences were debated but the debates were constructive not divisive.

The challenges the country has faced over the last four years have been extensive, complicated by a self-serving president and the overwhelming impact of the coronavirus pandemic and civil unrest across the country. Through it all Americans will gather their resolve in spite of the total absence of responsible governing from the White House and recognize how gravely they have been manipulated by lies.

Consider these three simple requests: Acknowledge each other. Respect each other. Speak truth.

Thank you, America.

SOURCE NOTES

Introduction

1. Nixon Oval Office Tapes: 886-008A
2. Tenure of Office Act of 1867
3. Fundraising organization affiliated with President Richard Nixon's 1972 reelection campaign.
4. A covert Special Investigations Unit established after the publication of the "Pentagon Papers" in June 1971.
5. Thomas, E. (2015). *Being Nixon: A Man Divided.* Random House.
6. New York Times Co. v. United States, 403 US 713.
7. Espionage Act of 1917 Pub. L. 65–24; currently found in 18 US Code § 793
8. File. 04unit-358.pdf. Richard Nixon Museum and Library, Yorba Linda, CA.
9. Pierre Salinger, former press secretary for President John F. Kennedy.
10. PEPFAR, https://www.hiv.gov/federal-response/pepfar-global-aids/pepfar.
11. Woodward, B. (2020). Rage. Simon & Schuster.
12. The disease caused by the SARS-CoV2 virus. COVID-19 stands for coronavirus disease of 2019.

13. Elliott, D. (2018). *Armageddon of a Different Order: Wake Up America*. iUniverse.
14. Dingell, J. (2018). *The Dean: The Best Seat in the House*. HarperCollins.

Chapter One

15. Retrieved July 16, 2020 from https://www.washingtonpost.com/graphics/politics/trump-claims-database
16. Answering a media question about the ongoing trade war with China on the White House driveway on Wednesday, August 21, 2019.
17. Interview on *Fox and Friends* on November 24, 2019.
18. Rick Perry campaign event July 22, 2015.
19. Pew Research Center survey conclusions published, March 25, 2020, *Most Americans don't see Trump as religious; fewer than half say they think he's Christian.*
20. Proverbs 6:16-19, King James Bible.
21. A deal, a reciprocal arrangement, when one party provides something and the other receives something in return
22. Rose Garden speech, June 16, 2020
23. White House briefing, April 6, 2020.
24. Retrieved April 13, 2020 from https://www.politico.com/f/?id=00000170-e50c-d588-ab77-ed5ff3310000.
25. Retrieved April 13, 2020 from https://obamawhitehouse.archives.gov/the-press-office/2017/01/16/readout-principal-level-transition-exercise
26. Huxley, A. (1932). *Brave New World*. Chatto & Windus.
27. Retrieved April 10, 2020 from https://abcnews.go.com/Politics/intelligence-report-warned-Covid-19-crisis-early-november-sources/story?id=70031273
28. World Threat Assessment of the Intelligence Community. Statement for the Record, January 29, 2019.
29. Retrieved March 20, 2020 from https://www.theatlantic.com/politics/archive/2020/03/pandemic-Covid-19-united-states-trump-cdc/608215/

30. World Economic Forum in Davos Switzerland; interview conducted by Joe Kernen, CNBC. Retrieved January 31, 2020 from https://www.cnbc.com/video/2020/01/22/watch-the-full-cnbc-interview-with-us-president-donald-trump-from-davos.html

31. *Wall Street Journal* opinion article; Luciana Borio, former member of disbanded National Security Council Pandemic Response Team; Scott Gottlieb, Food and Drug Administration Commissioner, 2017-2019.

32. Trump administration director of the Office of Trade and Manufacturing Policy.

33. Retrieved April 9, 2020 from https://www.axios.com/exclusive-navarro-deaths-Covid-19-memos-january-da3f08fb-dce1-4f69-89b5-ea048f8382a9.html

34. Trump remarks at a rally in Warren, MI.

35. WHO Situation Report-10, January 30, 2020.

36. Not a total ban at all. Foreign nationals who had traveled in China within the previous 14 days were temporarily banned from entering the US Exceptions were made for family members of US citizens and permanent residents. These individuals were allowed back after screening at ports of entry for an additional 14 days.

37. Notification of Arrival Restrictions Applicable to Flights Carrying Persons Who Have Recently Traveled From or Were Otherwise Present Within the People's Republic of China. Federal Register / Vol. 85, No. 23 / Tuesday, February 4, 2020 / Rules and Regulations; 19 CFR Chapter I, 49 CFR Chapter XII.

38. Sean Hannity interview with Trump on Fox News.

39. *The Fog of War: Eleven Lessons from the Life of Robert S. McNamara.* (2003) Sony Pictures.

40. Twitter, March 27, 2020.

41. Trump campaign rally in Manchester, New Hampshire, the first rally after his acquittal in the Senate impeachment trial.

42. Statements included in a Peter Navarro memo February 23, 2020. Retrieved April 9, 2020 from https://www.politico.com/news/2020/03/16/trump-inauguration-warning-scenario-pandemic-132797

43. Interview with CNBC; response to his opinion about the spread of the Covid-19.
44. White House press briefing.
45. CDC Telebriefing on Covid-19.
46. Campaign rally speech in Charleston, South Carolina
47. Fauci, A., Lane, H. & Redfield, R. (2020). Covid-19– Navigating the Uncharted. N Engl J Med, 382:1268-1269 DOI: 10.1056/NEJMe2002387
48. Statement to the media at Trump's visit to the CDC on March 7, 2020.
49. Twitter, March 9, 2020.
50. Retrieved April 10, 2020 from https://www.nytimes.com/2020/04/08/science/new-york-coronavirus-cases-europe-genomes.html
51. Address to the country from the Oval Office, March 12, 2020.
52. White House Rose Garden press conference.
53. Twitter, March 13, 2020.
54. White House press briefing.
55. Dr. Fauci interview on CNN April 12, 2020.
56. White House press briefing.
57. White House Press briefing, March 18, 2020.
58. Twitter, March 9, 2020.
59. Trump statements at White House press briefing, March 30, 2020. He stated as his source (unidentified) for his position, "was told to me by a tremendous power in the business."
60. White House press briefing
61. Twitter, April 11, 2020.
62. White House briefing, April 2, 2020.
63. White House briefing, April 13, 2020.

Chapter Two

64. Address by First Lady Michelle Obama, Democratic National Convention, July 25, 2016.
65. Trump interview with Jonathan Swan of *Axios*, August 3, 2020.
66. Michelle Obama address at the 2020 Democratic National Convention.

67. A video message from President Bush posted by the George W. Bush Presidential Center, May 2, 2020.
68. Twitter, May 3, 2020.
69. Fox News Town Hall, May 3, 2020.
70. The first lymph node to which cancer cells are most likely to spread from a primary tumor
71. Preamble to the Constitution of the United States of America
72. Speech at Basler Flight Service Oshkosh, WI August 24, 2020.
73. Statement during a White House briefing on jobs numbers, July 2, 2020.
74. © Paramount Pictures.
75. © 1993 Columbia Pictures.
76. Interview with the *Washington Post* on the topic of "Watergate: 25 Years Later," June 17, 1997.
77. US Constitution, Article I, Section 1.
78. Don McGahn, White House Counsel from January 2017 – October 2018.
79. Ruling November 25, 2019, by US District Court Judge Ketanji Brown Jackson.
80. News release from the office of House Speaker Nancy Pelosi, November 25, 2019.
81. News release from the office of House Speaker Nancy Pelosi, February 28, 2020.,
82. Charles Savage report in the *New York Times*, December 4, 2019.
83. Testimony before the House Judiciary Committee impeachment inquiry, December 4, 2019.

Chapter Three

84. From a sermon in Selma, AL March 8, 1965, the day after "Bloody Sunday" when civil rights protesters were attacked and beaten by police on the Edmund Pettus Bridge.
85. Drugs that target specific genes, proteins, or tissue that acts as a willing host to cancer cell proliferation.
86. Rucker, P. & Leonnig, C. (2020). *A Very Stable Genius: Donald J. Trump's Testing of America*. Penguin Press, p. 167.

87. Situation normal all f****d up
88. "Trump Advisor Stephen Miller Has Always Been This Way." *Los Angles Magazine*, October 30, 2018.
89. © John Landis, et al. *Animal House*. USA, 1978.
90. Retrieved March 26, 2020 from https://factba.se/transcript/donald-trump-press-conference-Covid-19-briefing-march-25-2020
91. Orwell, G. (1949). *1984*. Secker & Warburg.
92. Retrieved on March 26, 2020 from https://www.axios.com/trump-Covid-19-pandemic-playbook-7da0cf5b-1d83-438f-8111-57f955675dbc.html
93. Retrieved March 15, 2020 from https://www.politico.com/news/2020/03/13/trump-Covid-19-testing-128971
94. Director, NAID
95. White House Covid-19 Response Coordinator; previously served as the State Department's global AIDS coordinator
96. Kayleigh McEnany.
97. Kellyanne Conway.
98. White House Rose Garden press conference, March 13, 2020.

Chapter Four

99. https://www.merriam-webster.com/dictionary/strategy
100. Bolton, J. (2020). *The Room Where It Happened: A White House Memoir*. Simon & Schuster.
101. https://www.factcheck.org/2020/04/trumps-snowballing-china-travel-claim/
102. White House press briefing March 19, 2020.
103. May 3, 2020, ABC's "This Week."
104. Zithromax®, Pfizer Inc.
105. https://doi.org/10.1016/S0140-6736(20)31180-6, May 22, 2020.
106. White House press briefing, March 20,2020.
107. Eric Trump interview, Fox News May 16, 2020.
108. Retrieved May 12, 2020 from https://time.com/5835342/jared-kushner-time-100-talks-highlights/

109. Retrieved June 2, 2020 from https://www.vanityfair.com/news/2016/02/donald-trump-pope-francis-isis-vatican
110. Twitter, October 11, 2016
111. Meeting with health insurers Feb. 27, 2017
112. Surowiecki, J. (2004). *The Wisdom of Crowds*. Anchor Books: New York.
113. Press briefing July 16, 2020.
114. Twitter, May 16, 2020
115. Twitter, May 18, 2020
116. Federalist No. 51, "The Structure of the Government Must Furnish the Proper Checks and Balances Between the Different Departments," 1788, written by James Madison.
117. *Great News: Jared Kushner Doesn't Think the Coronavirus Is a "Health Reality*. Retrieved March 25, 2020 from https://www.vanityfair.com/news/2020/03/jared-kushner-coronavirus-no-biggie.
118. Twitter, July 30, 2020.
119. White House Press Conference, July 30, 2020.
120. Retrieved January 16, 2020 from https://www.eac.gov; survey report published in June 2017 and submitted to the 115th Congress in session.
121. Chiafalo v. Washington, No. 19-465; Colorado Department of State v. Baca, No. 19-518
122. 377 US 533 (1964).
123. 376 US 1 (1964)
124. Pew Research Center survey conclusions published March 25, 2020 survey, *Americans who primarily get news through social media are least likely to follow COVID-19 coverage, most likely to report seeing made-up news.*
125. Pew Research Center survey conclusions published January 29, 2020. *An oasis of bipartisanship: Republicans and Democrats distrust social media sites for political and election news*
126. Pew Research Center survey conclusions published February 20, 2020. *Few Americans are confident in tech companies to prevent misuse of their platforms in the 2020 election*

127. Specifically addressing immunity from liability created by section 230(c) of the Communications Decency Act (section 230(c). 47 USC. 230(c), May 28, 2020.
128. African American murdered by Minneapolis, MN police May 25, 2020.
129. Twitter, May 28, 2020
130. Twitter, May 29, 2020. "This Tweet violated the Twitter rules about glorifying violence. However, Twitter has determined that it may be in the public's interest for the Tweet to remain accessible."
131. In the 1960's when racial unrest was frequent, this language is attributed to the mayor of Miami, Walter Headley who boasted about using police brutality against rioters.
132. Sean Hannity interview, *GQ*, October 31, 2016.
133. Twitter, May 30, 2020
134. Statement by D.C. Mayor Muriel Browser, May 30, 2020.
135. Retrieved May 31, 2020 from https://wtop.com/dc/2020/05/protesters-in-d-c-converge-on-white-house-scuffle-with-secret-service-over-george-floyd-killing/
136. Twitter, May 30, 2020.
137. Pope John Paul's 2001 New Year's message.

Chapter Five

138. Open letter from Attorney General of Michigan Dana Nessel, May 20, 2020.
139. "I did not want to give the media the pleasure of seeing it." Comment to reporters following the Ford plant tour May 21,2020 in Ypsilanti, Michigan
140. Twitter, May 21, 2020
141. Retrieved May 21, 2020 from https://www.cnbc.com/2020/05/21/trump-doesnt-wear-coronavirus-mask-to-ford-plant.html
142. Twitter, May 31, 2020
143. As of Wednesday May 20, 2020, the day before Trump's visit to Ford.

144. Retrieved June 11, 2020 from https://thehill.com/homenews/campaign/502360-trump-rally-sign-up-includes-disclaimer-about-potential-covid-19-exposure

145. For the unfamiliar, "cover your ass."

146. Data from a panel conducted June 4-10, 2020, Pew Research Center

147. 2016 Republican Party Platform.

148. Speech at the Owens & Minor Distribution Center, Allentown, Pennsylvania, May 14, 2020.

149. Press gaggle outside the White House, May 21, 2020.

150. Reference the Diagnostic and Statistical Manual-V from the American Psychiatric Association.

151. Twitter, May 8, 2013.

Chapter Six

152. Rand, A. (1957). *Atlas Shrugged*. Random House: New York.

153. Speech to the National Association of Manufacturers, Washington, DC, August 29, 2017.

154. Woodward, B. (2018). Fear. Simon & Schuster.

155. Campaign rally in Phoenix, AZ July 11, 2015.

156. © 1992 "A Few Good Men," Columbia Pictures.

157. Song title from the musical, *Hamilton*, Act 2; book music and lyrics by Lin-Manuel Miranda.

158. Op-Ed, *Wall Street Journal*, June 16, 2020.

159. Retrieved May 28, 2020 from https://www.journalism.org.

160. CDC data as of September 27, 2020.

161. Founded in 2013 in response to the acquittal of teenager Trayvon Martin's accused murderer. The organization has grown to have an active global footprint.

162. Twitter, June 19, 2020

163. 18 U.S. Code § 2381.

164. Trump, M. (2020). *Too Much and Never Enough: How My Family Created the World's Most Dangerous Man*. Simon & Schuster.

165. Fox Business Network interview, August 8, 2020.

166. Virtual commencement address to 2020 Harvard University graduates by Martin Baron, *Washington Post* Executive Editor.

Chapter Seven

167. White House briefing, July 28, 2020.
168. White House briefing, July 28, 2020.
169. Best actress for her role in *Places in the Heart* (TriStar Pictures).
170. Montreal Cognitive Assessment test developed in 1996 by Ziad Nasreddine, MD validated to detect mild cognitive impairment.
171. Interview with Fox News medical correspondent Marc Siegel, July 22, 2020.
172. Retrieved June 19, 2020 from https://www.theguardian.com/commentisfree/2020/jun/15.
173. Pew Research Center, June 29, 2020. *Three Months In, Many Americans See Exaggeration, Conspiracy Theories and Partisanship in COVID-19 News.*
174. Gallup Poll, March-April 2020.
175. Twitter, January 22, 2017.
176. Statement delivered in the White House Rose Garden June 1, 2020.
177. Report issued August 18, 2020.
178. National Public Radio: Fresh Air Interview, April 2, 2018.

Epilogue

179. Likely the best known saying from legendary professional baseball player Satchel Paige.
180. From a poem by Dylan Thomas included in *In Country Sleep, And Other Poems*, 1952.
181. Codex Atlanticus, 42v; Kemp Marvellous 66.

www.ingramcontent.com/pod-product-compliance
Lightning Source LLC
Chambersburg PA
CBHW021906020426
42334CB00013B/509